Topics in Context

Shakespeare

Topics in Context   Shakespeare

Im Auftrag des Verlages herausgegeben von
Prof. Hellmut Schwarz, Mannheim
unter Mitarbeit von
Mervyn Whittaker, Bad Dürkheim

Erarbeitet von
Dr. Annette Leithner-Brauns, Dresden
Mervyn Whittaker, Bad Dürkheim
sowie
Dr. Paul Maloney, Hildesheim; Sabine Otto, Halle;
Angela Ringel-Eichinger, Bietigheim-Bissingen;
Geoff Sammon, Bonn

In Zusammenarbeit mit der Englischredaktion
Hartmut Tschepe (verantwortlicher Redakteur);
Dr. Ilka Soennecken (Bildredaktion);
Cornelia Hansch (Redaktionsleitung)

Layout und technische Umsetzung
Petra Eberhard Grafik Design, Berlin

Umschlaggestaltung
Klein & Halm Grafikdesign, Berlin

www.cornelsen.de

Dieses Themenheft wurde auf der Grundlage des Kapitels *Shakespeare*
des Oberstufenlehrwerks *Context 21* entwickelt.
Das *Teacher's Manual* (ISBN 978-3-06-033178-9) enthält eine Audio-CD
und eine DVD-ROM/Video (mit dem Video zum Schülerheft, inter-
aktiven Tafelbildern für Whiteboard und Beamer, Vorschlägen zur
Leistungsmessung und weiteren Materialien).

Die Links zu externen Webseiten Dritter, die in diesem Lehrwerk angegeben sind,
wurden vor Drucklegung sorgfältig auf ihre Aktualität geprüft. Der Verlag übernimmt
keine Gewähr für die Aktualität und den Inhalt dieser Seiten oder solcher, die mit
ihnen verlinkt sind.

1. Auflage, 1. Druck 2012

Alle Drucke dieser Auflage sind inhaltlich unverändert und können im Unterricht
nebeneinander verwendet werden.

© 2012 Cornelsen Schulverlage GmbH, Berlin

Das Werk und seine Teile sind urheberrechtlich geschützt.
Jede Nutzung in anderen als den gesetzlich zugelassenen Fällen bedarf der
vorherigen schriftlichen Einwilligung des Verlages.
Hinweis zu den §§ 46, 52 a UrhG: Weder das Werk noch seine Teile dürfen ohne eine
solche Einwilligung eingescannt und in ein Netzwerk eingestellt oder sonst öffentlich
zugänglich gemacht werden.
Dies gilt auch für Intranets von Schulen und sonstigen Bildungseinrichtungen.

Druck: Stürtz GmbH, Würzburg

ISBN 978-3-06-033127-7

 Inhalt gedruckt auf säurefreiem Papier aus nachhaltiger Forstwirtschaft.

Contents

Title	Text Form	Topic	Skills and Activities	page
Lead-in				
Shakespeare IWB	Photo; pieces of dialogue	Shakespearean language and theatre	Collecting information; making dialogues	6
Words in Context				
Shakespeare, His Theatre and His Time	Informative text, photo	The life and times of Shakespeare	Structuring and applying vocabulary	8
Part A Researching the Background to Shakespeare's Plays				
Introduction	Tag cloud; instructive text			10
A1 Shakespeare's Biography	Illustrations; photos; websites	Shakespeare's life, career and works	Doing research / project work; giving a presentation; preparing a quiz	11
A2 The Historical Background	Illustrations; photos; websites; non-fictional text	The time Shakespeare lived in	Doing research / project work; giving a presentation; preparing a quiz	11
A3 The Elizabethan World View	Illustrations; photos; websites	How the Elizabethans saw the order of the universe	Doing research / project work; giving a presentation; preparing a quiz	11
A4 Shakespeare's Theatre IWB	Illustrations; photos; websites	London playhouses; Shakespeare in performance	Doing research / project work; giving a presentation; preparing a quiz	11
Part B Drama				
B1 Love: A Midsummer Night's Dream CD	Drama (comedy; extract)	Confusion among lovers in a wood	Analysing drama; performing a dramatic scene; writing a text	12
B2 Power and Ambition: Julius Caesar CD	Drama (tragedy; extract)	The assassination of Caesar due to fear he may become a tyrant	Analysing speeches; performing a scene; analysing stylistic devices; writing an essay	14
B3 Revenge: Othello CD	Drama (tragedy; extract)	Iago sows suspicion in Othello's mind about Desdemona, Othello's wife	Analysing drama; performing a dramatic reading; speculating on plot; identifying conflict in plays and films	16

Contents

Title	Text Form	Topic	Skills and Activities	page
Part C Versions of Shakespeare				
C1 Comparing Two Shakespeare Productions	Documentary (extract); film (extract)	A 1970s stage version vs. a 21st-century film adaptation of *A Midsummer Night's Dream*	Viewing, analysing and comparing film extracts	18
C2 A Shakespeare Comic Strip	Comic	Iago sows suspicion in Othello's mind about Desdemona, Othello's wife	Working with comics	19
C3 Sonnets and the German Shakespeare	Poems; newspaper article (extract)	Two German translations of sonnet 29; how Shakespeare's sonnets might have come into existence	Reading poetry; mediating	20
Communicating across Cultures				
Dealing with Different Cultural Values	Shakespeare excerpts	cf. title	Dealing with cultural differences; analysing quotations; doing a role-play	23

Further Practice	
Words in Context	24
Part A: Researching the Background to Shakespeare's Plays [CD]	25
Part B: Drama	26
Part C: Versions of Shakespeare	28

Skills Support	
Skill 1 Doing research	31
Skill 2 Giving a presentation	32
Skill 3 Reading poetry	33
Skill 4 Reading/Watching drama	34
Skill 5 Writing an essay	35
Skill 6 Writing a comment	36
Skill 7 Writing a review	36

Active Vocabulary	37
vocabulary you should learn (from pages 6–22)	

Word Help	40
selected vocabulary from the accompanying audios and videos to assist comprehension	

Shakespearean English	42

Shakespeare's Work in German	43

Glossary	44
1 Drama/Play	44
2 Poetry	45
3 Stylistic devices	46

Acknowledgements	

Abbreviations and symbols

adj	adjective
AE	American English
BE	British English
c.	circa
cf.	confer, see
e.g.	(Latin) exempli gratia = for example
esp.	especially
etc.	(Latin) et cetera = and so on
fml	formal
i.e.	(Latin) id est = that is, in other words
infml	informal
jdm./ jdn.	jemandem/ jemanden
l./ll.	line/lines
n	noun
p./pp.	page/pages
sb.	somebody
sl	slang
sth.	something
vs.	(Latin) versus = against, in contrast to

CD 02	indicates that the listening text(s) can be found on the audio-CD in the Teacher's Manual (Track 2).
DVD	indicates that the videos can be found on the DVD-ROM/video in the Teacher's Manual.
IWB	indicates that interactive material (for use with an interactive whiteboard or a projector) can be found on the DVD-ROM/video in the Teacher's Manual.
EXTRA	indicates additional (optional) materials and tasks.
Webcode: TOP331277-09	is a code that can be entered at www.cornelsen.de/webcodes. This connects you directly to a specific website related to a section of this book. **Webcode:** TOP331277-09
sonnet*	indicates that the word or term (here: *sonnet*) is explained in the Glossary on pp. 44–48.
☆	indicates that the American English pronunciation follows.

Shakespeare

Welcome to the age of William Shakespeare. Before you learn more about his work, find out a little more about his language by trying to speak like someone from his time.

What dost thou[1] think?

Come hither, my dearest!

I will keep my word with thee.

Hence!

Aye[2], by my life.

Fare ye well!

Alackaday[3]! Out upon it!

What news, my sweet wench?

Thou lik'dst not that.

Hearken[4]!
What a flibbertigibbet[5] and hurly-burly[6] yonder!

Nay, yet there is more in this.

Fie, fie[7]! Shame on you!

Yes, honest!

Go!

Hang on, there is something else, isn't there?

You didn't like that, did you?

Over here, love!

Trust me.

What's up, dear?

Listen. What's going on over there?

What do you suppose?

No way, forget it!

That's so unfair!

Have a nice day.

[1] [ðaʊ]
[2] [aɪ]
[3] [əˌlækəˈdeɪ]
[4] [ˈhɑːkən]
[5] [ˌflɪbətiˈdʒɪbɪt]
[6] [ˈhɜːli ˌbɜːli]
[7] [faɪ]

1   IWB   Speaking like Shakespeare

a Your teacher will give you a slip of paper with either one of the Shakespearean phrases above or its modern English equivalent. Read it carefully and practise it quietly. Then go around in your classroom speaking your phrase and try to find your modern or Shakespearean counterpart.

b Speak your sentences in class so that everybody can become familiar with the phrases and their meaning. Ask for explanations if you need them.

c Together with your partner try to construct a setting where you could use five or six of the Shakespearean phrases and make a dialogue. You can add some modern phrases. Present the dialogue.

2   **EXTRA**   **Shakespeare's language**
Outline differences between Shakespearean and modern English. Look at aspects like individual words and their meanings, special word classes like pronouns, inflection, word formation and word order.

▶ Shakespearean English (p. 42)

3   **IWB**   **Shakespeare and you**
While dealing with the tasks below, collect all the information in a form that works for you (e.g. mind map, index cards, outline) and add more aspects as you work through this book.

a   The photo above shows a reconstructed Shakespearean theatre. Point out details that you find remarkable about it.

b   What (else) do you know about Shakespeare, his life and work, the time he lived in, etc.?

c   Give a personal comment on the question: What point is there in studying a dramatist who lived 400 years ago?

▶ Skill 6: Writing a comment (p. 36)

Words in Context

Shakespeare, His Theatre and His Time

> ⚠ **Trouble spot**
> **playwright** ['pleɪraɪt]
> = Dramatiker/in
> Not: ~~playwriter~~
> **writer** = Schreiber/in, Schriftsteller/in

Four hundred years after his death, William Shakespeare is still rated as the foremost playwright of the modern world. He wrote about three dozen plays – mainly comedies* and tragedies*, but also history plays which tell the story of his nation before the reign of his monarch, Elizabeth I.

The Elizabethan Age is often remembered as a golden age for its many achievements in the arts. However, England was struggling for peace and stability at home and against threats from foreign powers abroad. Religious, social, political and economic developments challenged society.

People were torn between a traditional world view and a more modern one; they generally accepted the Earth as the centre of the cosmos and the Church as the centre of life on Earth, but were keen to discover new truths beyond the old dogmas. Was Man master of his own fate or was his fate predetermined? What would happen if people left their place in society? Every year, men set out to discover new lands overseas, trading and making huge profits – all around, things were on the move. Shakespeare's drama* reflects this upheaval.

Shakespeare was a businessman, too, who invested in the theatre companies that produced his plays. Much more than today, theatre was a popular form of entertainment which could draw over 2500 spectators to a show, from aristocrats to apprentices. The playhouses were open to the sky and the platform stage had almost no scenery. It was surrounded on three sides by the groundlings (those standing on the ground) who took a lively part in the performance. So the actors (only men, as women were not allowed to perform on stage) had to use all their skills of speech, expression and gesture to hold the crowd's attention. Spectacular costumes and realistic props helped.

To make it difficult for rivals to steal the plays, actors were not given complete playscripts to learn their lines from, but used a transcript showing only their own role. Modern playscripts, of course, show the spoken text, i.e. the dialogue and monologues, for all the characters*. There are few stage directions* in Shakespeare's plays, and we are not sure if Shakespeare actually wrote them.

The works that 'the Bard' left behind have been translated into nearly every language and adapted for every kind of media, from comics and musicals to paintings and films. Millions of tourists visit the town of his birth and death, Stratford-upon-Avon, and the replica of his playhouse, the London Globe. His language may seem antiquated at first, but when his plays are performed – or just read aloud – his words come alive. Shakespeare's themes – ambition, revenge, love – are timeless.

> ⚠ **Trouble spot**
> **learn your lines/part** = seine Rolle lernen
> **role/part** = Rolle (die jd. spielt)
> **roll** = 1. Rolle (etwas Zusammengerolltes)
>   2. Brötchen

Shakespeare, His Theatre and His Time **Words in Context**

1 The world of theatre and drama
The text on p. 8 contains many words and phrases to do with these topics. Collect them and put them in a mind map; you might start with the subtopics suggested here:

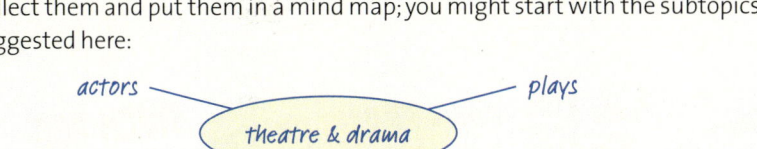

2 Definitions
Identify the words and phrases in the text which are defined here.

1. people watching an event
2. a movement used as a sign
3. instructions on how to perform
4. to work for something in the face of difficulties
5. a truth laid down and not to be questioned
6. a different identity which someone takes on in a play
7. fixed and unchangeable
8. two different words for a copy: a copy of a text – and a copy of a building

Pick out two or three other words from the text on the left and make a definition. Your partner has to guess the word.

3 Opposites
Use words and phrases from the text to complete these sentences:

1. The Elizabethan era was a golden age, but also a time of …
2. *As You Like It* is a comedy, while *Hamlet* …
3. Elizabethans did accept some traditional views, yet …
4. Some playhouses lost money, but others …
5. While a few private playhouses were indoors, the public ones …
6. Audiences were seldom bored, as the actors knew how to …
7. The actors were not trusted with a complete playscript, so …
8. Elizabethan theatre put elegant costumes and realistic props on stage, but …
9. Shakespeare's themes are timeless, though at first the language might seem …

4 Then and now:
What has changed since Shakespeare's age
– in the ways a play is performed?
– in the ways people see society and the world?
– in the role of theatre as entertainment?
You can start with phrases from the text: Playhouses used to be open to the sky, but modern theatres …

5 EXTRA Watching actors
When you watch actors – in a play, in a film, or on TV – what is it that helps most to make their performance convincing? Think about the elements in a performance. ● Language help

Language help
- cast
- speak your part
- interact with the other characters
- facial expression
- use of gesture

Webcode: TOP331277–09
▶ Further Practice 1–2 (p. 24)

Part A

Researching the Background to Shakespeare's Plays

- Put the titles of Shakespeare's plays shown above into three groups: 'comedies*', 'tragedies*' and 'history plays'.

Webcode: TOP331277-10

▶ Skill 2: Giving a presentation (p. 32)

In Part A there are four topics, A1–A4, with online material. Form four groups. Each group chooses one of the topics, researches online and then prepares a short presentation in the suggested form. Listen to the findings of the other groups. Finally, the class's knowledge of Shakespeare is tested in a quiz to which each group contributes three questions. The groups should let the teacher have their three questions before the presentations begin. Decide whether the quiz should be written or oral.

▶ Skill 1: Doing research (p. 31)

Doing research

1. Remember the aim of this activity: to pass on to your classmates the basic facts of your topic. You need to understand what you are presenting in order for your audience to understand it.
2. The Internet sites you are working with are designed for native English speakers. You will find some of the texts challenging, and you might not be able to do the tasks without a dictionary in book or online form.
3. The sites offer more information than you can pass on. You need to select carefully what is important and take written notes. Select interesting facts and search the Net for attractive illustrations: if the material appeals to you, it will appeal to your classmates.

Expanding vocabulary

Each group should collect 10–15 useful words and phrases from their work. Share the vocabulary in class and learn it.

Researching the Background to Shakespeare's Plays **Part A**

A1 Shakespeare's Biography

Your tasks are to:
- find out what is known about Shakespeare's life and career;
- find out about his works (for example, mention what forms of literature he wrote and give famous examples of each form).

Suggested form of presentation:
- a timeline featuring important dates, some illustrations and a selection of his best-known works

A2 The Historical Background

Your tasks are to:
- describe the time Shakespeare lived in – its society, economy, religion and politics;
- comment on what it was like to live in Shakespeare's London.

Suggested form of presentation:
- a large mind map with illustrations

A3 The Elizabethan World View

Your tasks are to:
- find out how the Elizabethans saw the order of the universe and what they meant by 'the chain of being', 'macrocosm and microcosm';
- explain how their world view influenced people's attitude to politics and society.

Suggested form of presentation:
- ten theses on the Elizabethan world view and how it influenced people's attitudes

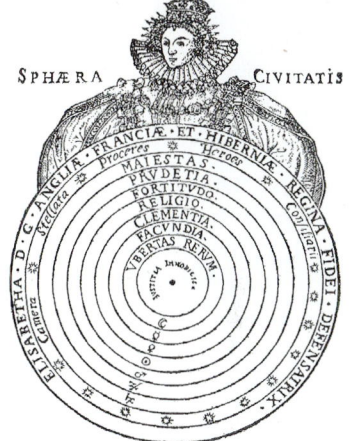

A4 IWB Shakespeare's Theatre

Your tasks are to:
- find out about the public playhouses in London;
- find out how plays were produced and financed, and what the laws were like for theatres;
- find out how plays were presented on stage.

Suggested form of presentation:
- Use this illustration of London, which shows the Globe at the very bottom, as the basis of your talk.

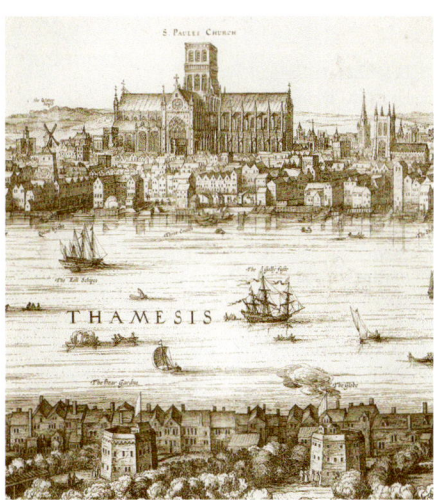

▶ Further Practice 3 (p. 25)

Part B

Drama

B1 　CD 02　Love: A Midsummer Night's Dream

THE PLOT SO FAR: On this midsummer night, Hermia and Lysander have run away into the forest together. They are deeply in love, but Hermia's father wants Demetrius to marry his daughter. So Demetrius is chasing them. He himself is being followed by Helena, who has fallen in love with him. In order to help the lovers, the spirits of the wood use a magical love-potion to make Demetrius love Helena instead of Hermia, thus creating two happy couples. But they only make things worse: Lysander accidentally gets a dose of the potion too and now he loves Helena instead of Hermia ...

- Study the diagram of the original relationships. Then add arrows to a copy of the second diagram to show who loves whom now. Explain what has changed.

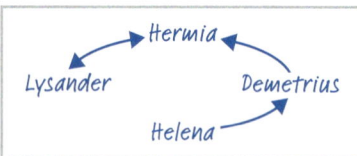 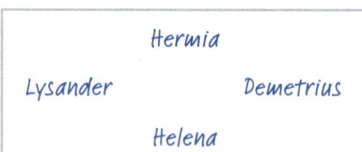

- Helena and Hermia have no idea why the men are behaving differently from before. Choose one of the girls and write down in about five sentences how she feels about the new situation they are all in.
  'I just don't get it! Only yesterday, Lysander was the sweetest ..., and now ... Hmm, I wonder if ...'

Listen to the text on the CD as you read the lines.

Lysander:	[to Hermia] Hang off, thou cat, thou burr! vile thing, let loose, Or I will shake thee from me like a serpent.
Hermia:	Why are you grown so rude? what change is this, Sweet love, –
Lysander:	Thy love! out, tawny Tartar, out!　　　5 Out, loathed medicine! hated potion, hence!
Hermia:	Do you not jest?
Helena:	Yes, sooth; and so do you.
Lysander:	Demetrius, I will keep my word with thee.
Demetrius:	I would I had your bond, for I perceive　　　10 A weak bond holds you: I'll not trust your word.
Lysander:	What! should I hurt her, strike her, kill her dead? Although I hate her, I'll not harm her so.
Hermia:	What! can you do me greater harm than hate? Hate me! wherefore? O me! what news, my love?　　15 Am not I Hermia? Are not you Lysander? I am as fair now as I was erewhile. Since night you lov'd me; yet, since night you left me: Why, then you left me, – O, the gods forbid! – In earnest, shall I say?　　　　　　　　　　20
Lysander:	Aye, by my life; And never did desire to see thee more.

Lysander [laɪˈsændə]
Hermia [ˈhɜːmiə]
Helena [ˈhelənə]
Demetrius [dɪˈmiːtriəs]

1 **burr** Klette
　vile hateful
2 **serpent** [ˈsɜːpənt] snake
5 **tawny** tancoloured, brown
6 **loathe sb./sth.** [ləʊð] hate sb./sth.
7 **jest** make fun
8 **sooth** [suːθ] honestly, truly
10 **bond** verbrieftes Dokument bzw. Band
12 **strike sb./sth.** hit sb./sth.
17 **fair** beautiful
　erewhile [eəˈwaɪl] before

	Therefore be out of hope, of question, of doubt;
	Be certain, nothing truer: 'tis no jest,
	That I do hate thee and love Helena. 25
Hermia:	O me! you juggler! you canker-blossom!
	You thief of love! what! have you come by night
	And stol'n my love's heart from him?
Helena:	Fine, i' faith!
	Have you no modesty, no maiden shame, 30
	No touch of bashfulness? What! will you tear
	Impatient answers from my gentle tongue?
	Fie, fie! you counterfeit, you puppet you!
Hermia:	Puppet! why, so: aye, that way goes the game.
	Now I perceive that she hath made compare 35
	Between our statures: she hath urg'd her height;
	And with her personage, her tall personage,
	Her height, forsooth, she hath prevail'd with him.
	And are you grown so high in his esteem,
	Because I am so dwarfish and so low? 40
	How low am I, thou painted maypole? speak;
	How low am I? I am not yet so low
	But that my nails can reach unto thine eyes.

From: *A Midsummer Night's Dream*, III, ii, 261–299

26 **juggler** trickster, false person
canker-blossom ['blɒsəm] Blütenfraß (Schädling)
30 **modesty** ['mɒdəsti] Sittsamkeit
maiden of a virgin
31 **bashfulness** shyness
33 **counterfeit** ['kaʊntəfɪt] fake
34 **why, so** ach, darum geht es!
36 **urg'd her height** hat auf ihre Größe gesetzt
37 **personage** ['pɜːsənɪdʒ] Erscheinung
38 **prevail** sich durchsetzen
39 **esteem** opinion
40 **dwarfish** ['dwɔːfɪʃ] wie ein Zwerg

> **Fact File**
> Shakespeare often uses elements of the **super-natural** in his plays. Some of his works include witches and magicians; in *Midsummer Night's Dream*, he creates a fairy kingdom as a kind of parallel world. His audience still believed in fairies and their influence on the lives of people.

1 Dealing with emotions
a Describe the way in which Lysander tells Hermia that he no longer loves her.
b Look at Hermia's reactions in ll. 3–20 and put them into everyday English. Note down the emotions that each of these reactions displays.

2 Working with characters*
What do we learn about Helena's and Hermia's height (ll. 35–43)? Explain how their height plays a part in their argument.

3 Performing a drama*
Act out one part of the scene*: In groups of four, choose either ll. 1–25 or 21–43. The text has no stage directions*, so you need to add instructions for the actors' speech, expressions and movements. Then practise speaking the lines before you act out the scene in front of the class.

4 EXTRA **Love**
'Love' can take on different forms. Collect some of the aspects of love you have come across in life, literature or film. Now choose five words that define the kind of love Shakespeare shows at work here. Write a paragraph using those five words.

5 Working with drama
a Every drama is based around conflict. List the conflicts that act as driving forces in this scene.
b EXTRA Speculate on how all the confusion in this scene will be sorted out in the end.

 Webcode: TOP331277-13

B2 CD 03 Power and Ambition: Julius Caesar

In *Julius Caesar*, we see a group of men including Brutus and Cassius plot against Caesar when he plans to become king of Rome. They fear he may become a tyrant. When he refuses to pardon Publius Cimber, a politician he has banished from the city, the conspirators assassinate Caesar. In the extract below, Brutus is talking to Cassius while, in the background, a crowd is urging Caesar to become king.

⚠ **Trouble spot**
tyrant ['taɪrənt], tyranny ['tɪrəni]

- Do you think there are circumstances where it can be justified to assassinate a tyrant? Consider events in recent history, and then discuss your viewpoints in class.
  Listen to the text on the CD as you read the lines.

From Act* I: *[Shout. Flourish.]*
Brutus: Another general shout!
          I do believe that these applauses are
          For some new honours that are heaped on Caesar.
Cassius: Why, man, he doth bestride the narrow world   5
          Like a Colossus; and we petty men
          Walk under his huge legs and peep about
          To find ourselves dishonourable graves.
          Men at some time are masters of their fates:
          The fault, dear Brutus, is not in our stars   10
          But in ourselves, that we are underlings.
          Brutus and Caesar: what should be in that 'Caesar'?
          Why should that name be sounded more than yours?
          Write them together, yours is as fair a name;
          Sound them, it doth become the mouth as well;   15
          Weigh them, it is as heavy; conjure with 'em,
          'Brutus' will start a spirit as soon as 'Caesar'.
          Now in the names of all the gods at once,
          Upon what meat doth this our Caesar feed,
          That he is grown so great? Age, thou art sham'd!   20
          Rome, thou hast lost the breed of noble bloods!
          When went there by an age since the great flood,
          But it was fam'd with more than with one man?

From Act III: *(Another day, at the Capitol)*
Cassius: Pardon, Caesar! Caesar, pardon!   25
          As low as to thy foot doth Cassius fall,
          To beg enfranchisement for Publius Cimber.
Caesar: I could be well mov'd if I were as you;
          If I could pray to move, prayers would move me.
          But I am constant as the northern star,   30
          Of whose true-fix'd and resting quality
          There is no fellow in the firmament.
          The skies are painted with unnumber'd sparks,
          They are all fire and every one doth shine,
          But there's but one in all doth hold his place.   35
          So in the world: 'tis furnished well with men,
          And men are flesh and blood, and apprehensive;

Brutus ['bruːtəs]
Cassius ['kæsiəs]
Caesar ['siːzə]

¹ **flourish** ['flʌrɪʃ ☆ 'flɜːrɪʃ] sound of trumpets
⁵ **bestride sth.** walk across sth.
⁶ **petty** unimportant
¹¹ **underling** Untergebene(r)
¹³ **sound sth.** call out
¹⁶ **conjure** ['kʌndʒə] make magic
¹⁷ **start sb./sth.** frighten sb./sth.
²¹ **breed** Zucht
²¹⁻²³ Rome has never allowed one single man to dominate an age.
²⁷ **enfranchisement** [ɪnˈfræntʃɪzmənt] Einbürgerung
³² **there is no fellow** there is nothing which is equal
³³ **spark** Funken
³⁶ **furnish sth.** etwas ausstatten
³⁷ **apprehensive** [ˌæprɪˈhensɪv] mit Sinnen begabt

	Yet in the number I do know but one
	That unassailable holds on his rank,
	Unshak'd of motion; and that I am he, 40
	Let me a little show it, even in this:
	That I was constant Cimber should be banish'd,
	And constant do remain to keep him so.
Cinna:	O Caesar –
Caesar:	Hence! Wilt thou lift up Olympus? 45
Decius:	Great Caesar –
Caesar:	Doth not Brutus bootless kneel?
Casca:	Speak, hands, for me!
[They stab Caesar.]	

From: *Julius Caesar*, I, ii, 133–156; III, i, 55–76

Cinna ['sɪnə]
Decius ['diːʃiəs]
Casca ['kæskə]

[39] **unassailable** that cannot be destroyed, moved
[40] **motion** movement
[42] **banish sb.** jdn. verbannen
[45] **Olympus** [ə'lɪmpəs] the mountain home of the ancient gods
[47] **bootless** in vain
[49] **stab sb.** jdn. erstechen

▶ Shakespeare's Work in German (p. 43)

1 Working with speeches
Examine the speeches of Cassius and Caesar:
a Point out the reasons Cassius has for opposing Caesar.
b Discuss whether Caesar's speech justifies Cassius's criticism.

2 Performing a drama
Depending on how you present these scenes, you can engage the audience's sympathy either for or against Cassius and Caesar. Try this:
a Speak Cassius's first nine lines to make him appear mean and spiteful.
b Speak Caesar's lines from 'The skies …' to '… to keep him so' (ll. 33–43) trying to make him appear reasonable and convincing.
c Then read both speeches the other way round, to change audience sympathy.

3 Working with stylistic devices*
Working in groups, study either Cassius's or Caesar's lines and point out the stylistic devices they use to move their listeners. Explain what effect these create. Put your findings in writing. ■ Language help

4 EXTRA **Examining the play in its context**
a Evaluate Caesar's message from the perspective of an Elizabethan. Use what you learned about the Elizabethan world view in **A3** (p. 11).
b Discuss whether there is a lesson in this play for a modern audience.

5 Analysing the conflict
As in the previous extract from a comedy*, this tragedy* is driven by conflict: take notes and write a short essay defining what form the conflict takes in this play.

Language help
- employ sth.
- make use of sth.
- compare sth. to sth. else
- stand for sth.
- evoke sth.
- portray sb./sth. as …
- address his listeners

▶ Skill 5: Writing an essay (p. 35)

B3 CD 04 Revenge: Othello

Many of Shakespeare's villains are driven by revenge. Iago is an ambitious soldier-servant to the 'Moor' Othello, a general in Venice. Iago had hoped to become Othello's lieutenant, but Michael Cassio was promoted in his place. Whether out of envy or just because of his natural hatefulness, Iago plots to make Othello believe that Cassio is having an affair with his wife, Desdemona. One day, as Othello watches Desdemona leave, Iago begins his work …

- Before you read the scene, discuss your own personal experiences: Where have you seen envy at work in people? Does it lead to a desire for revenge? Listen to the text on the CD as you read the lines.

Othello:	Excellent wretch! Perdition catch my soul
	But I do love thee! and when I love thee not,
	Chaos is come again.
Iago:	My noble lord, –
Othello:	What dost thou say, Iago? 5
Iago:	Did Michael Cassio, when you woo'd my lady,
	Know of your love?
Othello:	He did, from first to last: why dost thou ask?
Iago:	But for a satisfaction of my thought;
	No further harm. 10
Othello:	Why of thy thought, Iago?
Iago:	I did not think he had been acquainted with her.
Othello:	O! yes; and went between us very oft.
Iago:	Indeed!
Othello:	Indeed! ay, indeed; discern'st thou aught in that? 15
	Is he not honest?
Iago:	Honest, my lord?
Othello:	Honest! aye, honest.
Iago:	My lord, for aught I know.
Othello:	What dost thou think? 20
Iago:	Think, my lord!
Othello:	Think, my lord!
	By heaven, he echoes me,
	As if there were some monster in his thought
	Too hideous to be shown. Thou dost mean something: 25
	I heard thee say but now, thou lik'dst not that,
	When Cassio left my wife; what didst not like?
	And when I told thee he was of my counsel
	In my whole course of wooing, thou criedst, 'Indeed!'
	And didst contract and purse thy brow together, 30
	As if thou then hadst shut up in thy brain
	Some horrible conceit. If thou dost love me,
	Show me thy thought.
Iago:	My lord, you know I love you.

Othello [əʊˈθeləʊ]
Iago [iˈɑːgəʊ]
Cassio [ˈkæsiəʊ]
Desdemona [ˌdezdɪˈməʊnə]

1 **wretch** *(hier)* Geschöpf
perdition Verderben
6 **woo sb.** um jdn. werben
12 **acquainted** bekannt
15 **discern sth.** [dɪˈsɜːn] notice sth.
aught [ɔːt] *(old use)* anything
25 **hideous** [ˈhɪdɪəs] terribly ugly
28 **of my counsel** eingeweiht
30 **contract and purse your brow** [braʊ] die Stirn runzeln
32 **conceit** [kənˈsiːt] Vorstellung

Othello:	I think thou dost;	35
	And, for I know thou art full of love and honesty,	
	And weigh'st thy words before thou giv'st them breath,	
	Therefore these stops of thine fright me the more. [...]	
Iago:	For Michael Cassio,	
	I dare be sworn I think that he is honest.	40
Othello:	I think so too.	
Iago:	Men should be what they seem;	
	Or those that be not, would they might seem none!	
Othello:	Certain, men should be what they seem.	
Iago:	Why then, I think Cassio's an honest man.	45
Othello:	Nay, yet there's more in this.	

From: *Othello*, III, iii, 91–135

1 Understanding the text
a Outline Othello's opinion of Iago.
b Point out Iago's strategy as he makes Othello suspicious of Cassio.
- Language help

Language help
- pretend to ...
- arouse suspicion
- give hints about ...
- make sb. curious about ...

2 Working with characters
'When I love thee not, / Chaos is come again.' (ll. 2–3). Comment on this line with respect to Othello and what it tells us about him.

3 Performing a drama
a In groups of four, prepare the dialogue in the first half of the extract (up to 'too hideous to be shown', l. 25) for a dramatic reading. Before you start, study the text carefully and consider at which points you could insert a pause for better effect. Then read your different versions and decide which creates the most tension.
b Listen to the CD again and analyse how the professional actors interpret Shakespeare's text.

4 EXTRA Dealing with themes
Revenge and jealousy are at the heart of this drama. Identify the conflicts involving Othello, Iago, Desdemona and Cassio. Then, in pairs or groups, develop a plan of how the play might go on. Present your scenarios.

5 Identifying conflict
At the close of this section, collect all the dramatic conflicts you have identified in the three extracts on pp. 12–17. Many of these are timeless constellations that provide the drama of films and other plays you know. Try to identify where they occur in other settings.

▶ Further Practice 4–5 (pp. 26–27)

Part C

Versions of Shakespeare

C1 DVD Comparing Two Shakespeare Productions

When people go to see a Shakespeare play, some expect to see beautiful historical costumes, scenery designed to look realistic and actors trying to appear 'true to life'. Others say that it is best not to aim for an impression of reality but to use theatre's own 'language' to express what the dramatist meant.

1 Expectations
What do you expect a Shakespeare play to look like on stage?

▶ Skill 4: Reading/Watching drama (p. 34)

▶ Word Help (pp. 40–41)

2 Comparing performances
a You have read one scene* from *A Midsummer Night's Dream*. The play continues with the lovers getting lost in a forest on this midsummer's night, a forest full of elves and fairies who play tricks on them until they hardly know who they are and who belongs to whom. Now watch two clips from different versions of *A Midsummer Night's Dream*: one from a documentary about a British stage version from 1970, and one from a recent BBC production. Watch first to get an idea of what is going on. Then watch again and analyse the clips by filling in a copy of the table on the right.

Look out for …	Stage version	BBC version
costume	? ? ? ? ?	? ? ? ? ?
scenery	? ? ? ? ?	? ? ? ? ?
sound	? ? ? ? ?	? ? ? ? ?
effects	? ? ? ? ?	? ? ? ? ?
props	? ? ? ? ?	? ? ? ? ?
lighting	? ? ? ? ?	? ? ? ? ?
acting, movement	? ? ? ? ?	? ? ? ? ?
language used	? ? ? ? ?	? ? ? ? ?

b Which version do you like better? Justify your choice.
c Assess which is closer to Shakespeare.

3 Directing a play
In groups do one of the following tasks showing how you imagine your own production of Shakespeare:
a How would you present the fairies on your school stage?
b Suggest different ways of staging Julius Caesar's assassination.

Versions of Shakespeare Part C

C2 A Shakespeare Comic Strip

The following comic version of Othello *depicts the scene that you read in* **B3** (pp. 16–17).

From: *William Shakespeare's Othello*, Illustrated by Oscar Zarate. London: Can of Worms Press, 2005

Part C Versions of Shakespeare

Language help
- modernize sth.
- old-fashioned
- contemporary
- use a different medium
- appeal to different groups of people
- impact on the audience
- illustrations
- props
- close-ups

▶ Further Practice 6–8 (pp. 28–30)

1 Examining the comic
a Choose one frame of the comic that appeals to you and describe it.
b Analyse the special devices the comic uses.
c How does the visualization change the effect of the drama* text?

2 Discussion
'I believe we should only allow the real Shakespeare. All these other versions are not the true original!' Discuss (You can use Think/Pair/Share).
- Language help

C3 Sonnets and the German Shakespeare

Besides writing nearly 40 plays, Shakespeare also wrote a sonnet* cycle consisting of more than 150 sonnets about a poet* called Will, his handsome young friend, his loved one (the 'Black Lady') and a rival poet.

- Look at this picture of Shakespeare from the cover of *ZEITmagazin* (1987) by Michael Mathias Prechtl and describe what – according to the images in the picture – he writes about in his poetry.

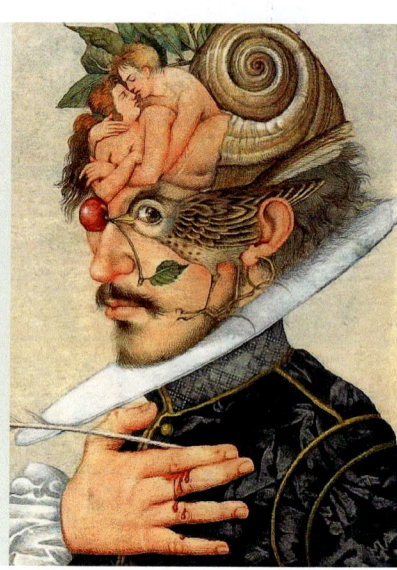

Sonnet 29

When in disgrace with Fortune and men's eyes,
I all alone beweep my outcast state,
And trouble deaf heaven with my bootless cries,
And look upon myself, and curse my fate,
Wishing me like to one more rich in hope, 5
Featur'd like him, like him with friends possess'd,
Desiring this man's art, and that man's scope,
With what I most enjoy contented least;
Yet in these thoughts myself almost despising,
Haply I think on thee, and then my state, 10
Like to the lark at break of day arising
From sullen earth, sings hymns at heaven's gate;
For thy sweet love remem'br'd such wealth brings
That then I scorn to change my state with kings.

¹ **disgrace** bad favour
³ **bootless** useless
⁴ **curse sth.** etwas verfluchen
⁶ **featur'd like him** looking like him
¹⁰ **haply** by chance; happily
¹² **sullen** bad-tempered
¹⁴ **scorn to do** *(fml)* refuse to do

▶ Skill 3: Reading poetry (p. 33)

1 Analysis
a Compare the speaker's* mood at the beginning and at the end of the poem*. Then divide the poem into sections, giving each a heading.
b Analyse the structure of the poem. In what way do structure and form underline its content and the above-mentioned feelings?
c What concept of love is depicted in the sonnet? Compare it with the different forms of love you have encountered in the course of this book.

▶ Skill 1: Doing research (p. 31)

2 EXTRA Research
Research the literary history of sonnets in Europe from their birth in Italy to Shakespeare, examining how Shakespeare's sonnets fit into this tradition.

Versions of Shakespeare Part C

3 Examining translations

Shakespeare's plays and sonnets have frequently been translated into German. Look at these two versions of Sonnet 29.

▶ Shakespeare's Work in German (p. 43)

Ich hab kein Geld und auch kein Ansehn mehr, ich wein' alleine, freund- und heimatlos. Der Himmel hört's nicht, schrei ich noch so sehr. Seh' ich mich so, verfluche ich mein Los. 5 So hoffnungsvoll wie jener möchte ich sein, möchte eines Freund', des anderen Gesicht, so kunstvoll, so erfolgreich möchte ich sein, Was ich besitze, das gefällt mir nicht. Wenn meine Selbstachtung schon fast zerbricht, 10 denk' ich zum Glück an dich: Das macht mich froh, und wie die Lerche, wenn der Tag anbricht, sing ich dann Hymnen an das Himmelstor.	Wenn ich, von Gott und Menschen übersehn, Mir wie ein Ausgestoßener erscheine, Und, da der Himmel nicht erhört mein Flehn, Dem Schicksal fluche und mein Loos beweine: Wünsch ich an Hoffnungen so reich zu sein 5 Wie Andere, vielbefreundet, hochgeboren – In Kunst, in Freiheit Manchen gleich zu sein, Unfroh bei dem was mir das Glück erkoren. Zur Selbstverachtung treibt mich fast mein Sorgen, Doch denk ich Dein, ist aller Gram besiegt – 10 Der Lerche gleich' ich dann, die früh am Morgen Helljubelnd auf zum goldnen Himmel fliegt.

a One of the translations was published by Friedrich Bodenstedt in 1866, the other is by a contemporary translator called Markus Marti. State who wrote which and justify your answer.

b Identify five aspects in the two texts that are translated differently. Evaluate which version is closer to the original.

4 Creative writing

As you may have noticed, the last two lines (the rhyming couplet*) are missing in both German versions. Together with a partner make your own German version of them.

 **Webcode:** TOP331277-21

5 Mediation

While researching information on Shakespeare's sonnets, you come across the following article. Sum up its main aspects for a presentation in class.

Vor vierhundert Jahren passierte vielleicht Folgendes: Ein Mensch, der William Shakespeare nahestand, stahl sich in des Dichters Arbeitszimmer in London und entwendete dort ein Bündel Papiere. 154 kürzere Gedichte hatte Shakespeare abends, wenn er von den Proben
5 nach Hause kam, auf große weiße Bögen gekritzelt, dazu noch ein längeres Poem, das er „A Lover's Complaint" nannte. Eigentlich wollte der Dichter den Kram gar nicht veröffentlichen, jedenfalls nicht gleich, aber sein Freund, dieser falsche Hund – dem wir Nachgeborenen übrigens gar nicht dankbar genug sein können – hatte deutlich andere Pläne.
10 Hinter dem Rücken des Meisters trug er das Manuskript zu einem Drucker, und der machte ein Buch im handlichen Quartoformat daraus. […]

Jedenfalls trug dieser Literaturdiebstahl dem Dieb eine der geheimnisvollsten Widmungen ein, seit Menschen mit Büchermachen beschäftigt sind: an einen „Mr. W. H.", der „the only begetter" der Gedichte
15 genannt wird. Diese Bezeichnung „begetter" ließe sich als „Erzeuger", „Beschaffer" deuten.

```
TO.THE.ONLIE.BEGETTER.OF.
THESE.INSVING.SONNETS.
Mr.W.H. ALL.HAPPINESSE.
AND.THAT.ETERNITIE.
PROMISED.
BY.
OVR.EVER-LIVING.POET.
WISHETH.
THE.WELL-WISHING.
ADVENTVRER.IN.
SETTING.
FORTH.

            T. T.
```

21

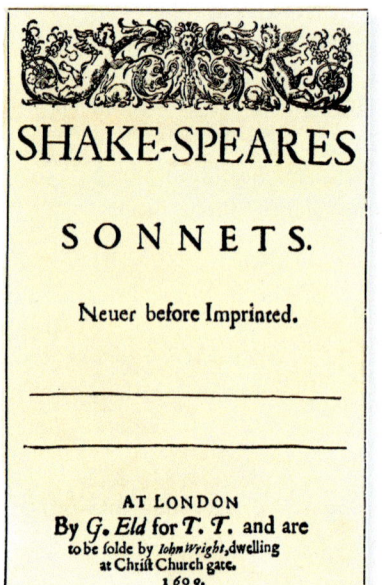

Oder es war alles ganz anders. Vielleicht wollte Shakespeare seine Sonette veröffentlicht sehen und trug sie selbst zum Drucker, die manchmal etwas seltsame Reihenfolge stammt von ihm, und mit der geheimnisvollen Widmung ist der englische Adelige Henry Wriothesley gemeint. Kann aber auch sein, dass „W. H." keck für „Will Himself" steht. Wir wissen es nicht und werden es nie herauskriegen. Fest steht nur, dass 1609 in den Buchläden [...] in London ein Büchlein auf den Markt kam: „SHAKE-SPEARES SONNETS. Neuer before Imprinted." (nie zuvor gedruckt) stand auf dem Titelblatt. Das Ding kostete nicht mehr als eine Handvoll Pennys und der Autor war damals schon berühmt. 1609 war William Shakespeare genau 45 Jahre alt, nach damaligen Maßstäben: ein alter Mann (sieben Jahre später starb er zuhause in Stratford-upon-Avon). [...]

Jeder gebildete Mensch wusste damals ungefähr, was man von einer Sammlung von Sonetten zu erwarten hatte: Ein Ich schwärmt eine unerreichbare Geliebte an. Diese Geliebte wird mit den Sternen verglichen, die zwar unerreichbar sind, uns hienieden aber Halt und Orientierung geben. Immer edler wird das Schwärmen und immer geistiger die Liebe, bis sie eigentlich nur noch das Ideal der Schönheit meint. Solche gebildeten Leser sollten sich bei der Lektüre von Shakespeares Liebesgedichten sehr wundern. Erste Überraschung: Hier wird keine Frau angesprochen, angehimmelt, angeschwärmt, sondern ein junger Mann von edlem Stand (jener Henry Wriothesley, von dem oben die Rede war? Keine Ahnung). Der Dichter drängt den jungen Mann, endlich ein Kind zu machen: Los schon, sorge für Nachwuchs, sagt er, denn du bist schön, aber deine Schönheit wird vergehen – siehst du, der Winter kommt schon, und er wird dir Furchen in deine Stirn graben –, also sorge dafür, dass deine Schönheit in deinem Sohn überlebt. [...] Deine Schönheit wird vergehen, sagt der Dichter, der Sensenmann holt dich gleich, aber hier, in meinem Gedicht, bist und bleibst du unsterblich. [...]

Und dann betritt eine neue persona dramatis die Bühne: eine dunkle Dame, eine wilde Schöne, die den Dichter schier um den Verstand bringt, denn sie lockt ihn in die Hölle der Begierden. Übrigens treibt sie es nicht nur mit ihm, sondern offenbar auch mit dem jungen Adeligen. Das macht den Dichter nicht so sehr eifersüchtig, als vielmehr wütend [...]. Seinen schmallippigen Sarkasmus aber spart sich Shakespeare für einen Nebenbuhler im Hintergrund auf, einen Schatten, einen Dichter, der seinen Männerschwarm mit verlogenen Metaphern überhäuft. [...]

Nicht alle 154 Sonette, die Shakespeare schrieb, treffen uns heute darum noch mit derselben unverminderten emotionalen Wucht [...]. Aber beim Blättern findet der Leser dann doch immer wieder Verse, die ihn zur Ruhe kommen lassen.

From: Hannes Stein, 'So lange Menschen atmen ...', *Die Welt*, 28 October 2009

TOPIC TASK
My Shakespeare!
What is your own personal image of Shakespeare after working through this book? Find a form to express what you think about the Bard now. You could make a collage, a cartoon, a mind map or whatever you think suitable. Include text as well as illustrations.

Communicating across Cultures

Dealing with Different Cultural Values

Culture has often been defined as 'the way we do things around here'. This can cause difficulties in communication and interaction between different 'cultures', as what is considered acceptable behaviour in one culture may be unacceptable in another.

1 Dealing with cultural differences

Together with a partner, look at the situations below. Put yourself in the position of someone faced with these situations: try to apologize and explain your mistake by referring tactfully to how things are done in your culture. Act out your dialogue in front of the class. • Language help

1. You are in China at a birthday party, and insist your host should unwrap your present. In China, one never unwraps presents that have been brought to a party until after the event, for fear of embarrassing the guests.
2. You are shocked by an Indian friend who has a swastika• on his wall. Your friend explains that in Hindu culture the swastika denotes positive things like peace and harmony.
3. You are on a holiday trip to a southern European country and want to visit a religious building. You are reprimanded because you are wearing a sleeveless top and shorts that show your knees.

Language help
- I'm sorry, no offence was intended
- how silly/thoughtless of me
- No, really, it was my fault ...
- I didn't mean to ...
- please forgive me for ...
- I really meant no harm, but I just took it for granted that ...
- back home, you see, we always ...

• swastika ['swɒstɪkə] Hakenkreuz

2 Old-fashioned values

Taking into consideration what you have learned about Shakespearean times, imagine an Elizabethan and a modern person meet and discuss the values revealed in these lines. Act out the dialogue (in modern English).

Egeus (about his daughter Hermia who doesn't want to do what he wants):
　As she is mine I may dispose of her
　Which shall be either to this gentleman
　Or to her death.   (*A Midsummer Night's Dream*, I, i, 42–44)
5　Othello after having killed Desdemona because of false accusations:
　A honourable murderer, if you will;
　For nought I did in hate, but all in honour.   (*Othello*, V, ii, 297–298)
　King Richard (fearing for his power and position as a king):
　The breath of worldly men cannot depose
10　The deputy elected by the Lord.   (*Richard II*, III, ii, 56–57)
　Katherina about women and their behaviour:
　I am asham'd that women are so simple
　To offer war where they should kneel for peace;
　Or seek for rule, supremacy, and sway
15　When they are bound to serve, love, and obey.   (*The Taming of the Shrew*, V, ii, 161–164)
　Lady Capulet urging the death penalty for the killer of her cousin:
　I beg for justice, which thou, Prince, must give:
　Romeo slew Tybalt, Romeo must not live.   (*Romeo and Juliet*, III, i, 182–183)

2 **dispose of sb.** get rid of sb.
7 **nought** nothing
9 **depose** remove from office
10 **deputy** ['depjuːti] substitute
14 **supremacy** [suːˈpreməsi]/ **sway** power
18 **slew** killed

⚠ **Trouble spot**
must not = darf nicht
Not: ~~muss nicht~~

3 EXTRA **Understanding intercultural communication**

On the basis of your conversations write down three 'golden rules' of intercultural communication.

23

Further Practice

Words in Context
Shakespeare, His Theatre and His Time

1 Talking about the theatre ▶ Words in Context, pp. 8–9
Complete the text with highlighted words from 'Words in Context'.

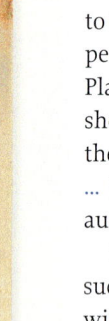

A play is written by a … [1], like William Shakespeare for example. It is usually divided into acts and scenes, with the main … [2] being introduced to the audience in Act* 1. A play is mostly a series of … [3] between two or more people, but sometimes there are also … [4], which only involve one person. Playscripts usually contain … [5], which tell the actors when and where they should enter or leave the … [6]. They may also describe the … [7] or facial … [8] they are supposed to use to show their emotions. Actors need to … [9] their … [10] by heart so that they can play their … [11] properly and hold the audience's … [12].

Two major types of dramas* are … [13], whose aim is to make people laugh, such as Shakespeare's *A Midsummer Night's Dream*, and … [14], which often deal with a difficult conflict or situation, e.g. *Hamlet*. The main … [15] in *Romeo and Juliet* is the love affair between two children whose families are enemies. Another important category of Shakespeare's plays is the … [16], for example *Richard II*, or *Henry V*, which are about English kings.

2 What did he say? ▶ Words in Context, pp. 8–9
John Kesprott has a problem with long words. Which words from 'Words in Context' does he mean? Write out the 'problem words' along with the corrected versions.

1 The 20th century was a time of great upveehal, with two world wars and communist relovutions.
2 I can't stand it when somebody's mobile rings during the permorphance.
3 Have you been to the Globe? It's a pecrilla of Shakespeare's theatre.
4 In the Billy Peethan Age people were beginning to question old mogdas and ankitwated thinking.
5 Hamlet is seen as someone whose fate is pretimernded. But is that true?
6 Shakespeare's time, with its many ameachvents in the arts, was the Olden Gage of the English theatre.
7 I really don't like the liar dog in some of these modern plays.

Shakespeare's Globe Theatre on the south bank of the River Thames in London

Inside the Globe

Part A
Researching the Background

3 Shakespeare in Stratford CD 05–06 ▶ A1–A4, p.11

You are going to hear a recording by a British tourist organization with interviews about various aspects of Shakespeare in Stratford-upon-Avon.

▶ Word Help (p.41)

Tip
The language in this listening text is fairly easy to follow. One difficulty is that the recording involves quite a lot of different speakers. The questions will help to guide you through this.

a Listen to part 1 and choose the correct answers.
1 The Royal Shakespeare Theatre
 a has just closed.
 b is being renamed 'the Memorial Theatre'.
 c was originally founded by Shakespeare.

2 Which of the following theatres has or will have a thrust stage, i.e. a platform stage? *(more than one answer is possible)*
 a The Swan Theatre. b The Courtyard Theatre.
 c The new Royal Shakespeare Theatre.

3 The commentator says that the advantage of the thrust stage is that
 a it is much cheaper than the traditional stage.
 b the audience is much closer.
 c it was the type of stage used by Shakespeare.

4 The Courtyard Theatre *(more than one answer is possible)*
 a seats 1000 people. b has seats for 2000 people.
 c is only a temporary theatre.
 d is a permanent theatre which will take four years to build.
 e is located in the courtyard of the house Shakespeare was born in.
 f is being used to help with the planning of the new RST.

b Listen to part 2 and choose the correct answers.
1 Shakespeare
 a has always been held in high esteem.
 b was never held in such high esteem as in the 1960s.
 c hasn't always been regarded so highly.

2 In the 17th and 18th centuries his style was regarded as rather
 a good. b messy. c poor.

3 In the 19th century Shakespeare was seen as
 a much too rude, maybe pessimistic.
 b far too old and pessimistic.
 c far too modern and optimistic.

4 The last speaker claims that Shakespeare is a great poet* because
 a he wrote very movingly at an important time in England's history.
 b he wrote strong plays for a strong people.
 c he wrote very bravely at a very difficult time.

5 He adds that
 a Shakespeare turned chaos and darkness into beauty and coherence.
 b Shakespeare showed audiences the beauty of darkness.
 c Shakespeare turned coherence into chaos to shock his audiences.

William Shakespeare's birthplace

The Royal Shakespeare Theatre on the River Avon

Part B
Drama

▶ Shakespearean English (p. 42)

4 A changing language ▶ B1–B3, pp. 12–17
a Complete the table below, giving the modern English or German equivalents of the excerpts listed. They are taken from **B1–B3**.

	Shakespeare's English	Modern English	Modern German
1	Upon what meat doth this our Caesar feed, That he is grown so great? *Julius Caesar*, p. 14, ll. 19–20	What meat does this our Caesar feed upon that he has grown so great?	Von welchem Fleisch ernährt sich unser Cäsar, dass er so groß geworden ist?
2	Why are you grown so rude? *A Midsummer Night's Dream*, p. 12, l. 3	? ? ? ? ? ? ? ? ? ? ? ?	Warum bist du so unfreundlich geworden?
3	Do you not jest? *A Midsummer Night's Dream*, p. 12, l. 7	Aren't you joking?	? ? ? ? ? ? ? ? ? ? ? ?
4	What dost thou say, Iago? *Othello*, p. 16, l. 5	? ? ? ? ? ? ? ? ? ? ? ?	? ? ? ? ? ? ? ? ? ? ? ?
5	… discern'st thou aught in that? *Othello*, p. 16, l. 15	? ? ? ? ? ? ? ? ? ? ? ?	… fällt dir daran etwas auf?
6	'tis no jest, That I do hate thee and love Helena. *A Midsummer Night's Dream*, p. 13, ll. 24–25	? ? ? ? ? ? ? ? ? ? ? ?	? ? ? ? ? ? ? ? ? ? ? ?
7	… he doth bestride the narrow world Like a Colossus; *Julius Caesar*, p. 14, ll. 5–6	? ? ? ? ? ? ? ? ? ? ? ?	… er geht auf dieser kleinen Welt wie ein Koloss;

Scene from 'Julius Caesar'

b Imagine William Shakespeare has landed in the 21st century in a time machine. He needs money, so he has decided to write a play. Help him to modernize his English.
Oswald: Why does your Grace …?

ACT II, SCENE 3 (A room in the palace)

[Enter Oswald and Sir Edgar]
Oswald: Why looks your Grace so seriously today?
Edgar: The night was storm-toss't, Strange cries were heard, 5 and ghosts, men say, Did walk abroad.
Oswald: Aye, some say the earth was feverous and did shake. Thus do the Fates betray 10 the evil that men seek to hide. Goes the king hence today?
Edgar: I'faith, before the clock hath yet struck two. 15
Oswald: Ride you with him this afternoon?
Edgar: I do, if all goes well.
[Enter a servant]
Servant: O horror! Horror! 20
Oswald: What's the matter?
Servant: Know ye not the news? The king, the king is dead! Most foully murdered while he was yet abed! 25

c **EXTRA** Write a paragraph highlighting some differences between modern English and Shakespeare's use of English. Find examples from exercises **4a** and **4b** of the following changes:
- form of the present perfect
- form of questions
- use of *do*

Can you find any similarities to German?

Shakespeare uses 'be' to form ... • **Language help 1**

Language help 1
- a regular form
- correspond to ...
- form a question / a statement / the present perfect
- Shakespeare's use of ...
- similar
- varied

5 Relationships and status ▶ B1–B3, pp. 12–17

a Your English friend Steve is learning German, but he can't understand the difference between 'du' and 'Sie'. Write an email to him, outlining when each form should be used. Use the examples given in 1–6 below, adding a German translation for each sentence.
1. Can you lend me your pen? (said to a stranger)
2. How old are you? (said to a child)
3. I love you.
4. Do you fancy a drink? (said to a friend)
5. Can you lend me your car? (said to a parent)
6. Do you know where the train station is? (said to a policeman)

Dear Steve, You asked me about 'du' and 'Sie'. Basically we use ...
• **Language help 2**

Tip
There is only one form of address *(you)* in English, so German expressions like 'duzen' and 'siezen', or 'jemandem das Du anbieten' cannot be easily translated into English. *Call somebody 'du'* doesn't make any sense to an English speaker who doesn't know any German. The best equivalents are *use the familiar form* or *use the polite form*. Note that *be on first-name terms with sb.* no longer has the same meaning as 'duzen', as English speakers use first names when talking to each other in almost all situations.

Language help 2
- be the same age
- close friend
- know sb. well
- (use) the familiar form
- (use) the polite form

b In Shakespeare's day there were also two forms of address: *thou* and *you*. Copy and complete the lines below from *Othello* (1) and *Midsummer Night's Dream* (2–3) with *you, thou* (subject pronoun), *thee* (object pronoun), and *thy* (possessive determiner).

1. a *Othello:* But I do love ...! and when I love ... not, /
       Chaos is come again.
    b *Othello:* What dost ... say, Iago?
    c *Othello:* Why of ... thought, Iago?
    d *Iago:* My lord, ... know I love ... .

2. a *Lysander:* Hang off, ... cat, ... burr! [...] /
       Or I will shake ... from me like a serpent.
    b *Hermia:* Do ... not jest?

3. a *Hermia:* O me! ... juggler! ... canker-blossom! /
       ... thief of love!
    b *Helena:* Have ... no modesty, no maiden shame, /
       No touch of bashfulness?
    c *Hermia:* How low am I, ... painted maypole?

Scene from 'Othello', 1965

c **EXTRA** Explain which forms Othello and Iago (pp. 16–17) use to address each other and why. Then do the same with Lysander and Hermia (p. 12) and Hermia and Helena (p. 13). The Tip box will help you.

Tip
Forms of address in 16th-century England were complex. In general, *thou/thee/thy* (or *thine* before a vowel or 'h') was used by higher-status persons to lower-status ones, whereas *you/your* was used by lower-status people to those above them in social rank, e.g. servants to their lord, children to parents and even wives to husbands. People of high status used *you* to each other, but people of low status used *thou*. However, people who would normally use *you* to each other switched to *thou* in very emotional situations.

Part C
Versions of Shakespeare

6 Themes of drama ▶ C2, pp. 19–20

a Shakespeare's dramas are based on emotional conflicts. Copy and complete the table with words related to these themes. You will find them all in **B1–C2** (pp. 12–20).

Verb	Noun	Adjective
love	love	lovely, loving
—	??????	ambitious
—	??????	angry
????	envy	??????
hate	??????	??????
—	??????	honest
—	??????	jealous
avenge	??????	vengeful
suspect	??????	??????

Scene from 'Othello', 2009

b Complete the text with suitable words from **6a**. Sometimes more than one answer is possible.

One of the many themes in *Othello* is … [1]: Iago is an … [2] servant who hopes for more power by becoming Othello's lieutenant. However, Othello promotes Michael Cassio in his place. Iago is naturally … [3] and is driven by his … [4] of Cassio. He decides to … [5] himself on Cassio by making Othello … [6] of him. Iago sows doubts in Othello's mind about Cassio's … [7], suggesting that he does not always tell the truth and making Othello … [8] that Cassio is having an affair with Desdemona. Othello's … [9] that Cassio is in … [10] with Desdemona becomes so great that Iago's plans for … [11] lead to a tragic end.

7 'The most unkindest cut of all' ▶ C2, pp. 19–20

Look at these excerpts from Shakespeare. Write down the modern English version of the comparative or superlative forms, 'correcting' Shakespeare's usage where necessary.

1. *Antony:* This was the most unkindest cut of all.
   (*Julius Caesar*, Act III, Scene 2)
   This was the … cut of all.
2. *Coriolanus:* Ay; 'tis an honester service than to meddle[1] with thy mistress.
   (*Coriolanus*, Act IV, Scene 5)
   Yes. It's … work than meddling with your mistress.
3. *Duke:* To vouch this, is no proof,
            Without more certain and more overt[2] test … (*Othello*, Act I, Scene 3)
   To assure this is not proof, without a … test.
4. *Steward:* I was very late more near her than I think she wished me …
   (*All's Well That Ends Well*, Act I, Scene 3)
   Only recently I was … her than I think she wanted me to be.

[1] **meddle with sb.** sich mit jdm. einlassen
[2] **overt** [əʊˈvɜːt, ˈəʊvɜːt] offen

Part C **Further Practice**

8 Problems with Shakespeare ▶ C2, pp. 19–20

a Look at the photo on the right, which is from a modern production of *The Merchant of Venice*. Discuss whether you find it suitable as a modern version of a Shakespeare play.

b The following article by Susan Bassnett from the British quality newspaper *The Independent* examines why it is difficult even for many English-speaking people to understand Shakespeare today.

The Merchant of Venice

Shakespeare's in danger.
We have to act now to avoid a great tragedy.

The other day I took my family to see one of my favourite Shakespeare plays. You'll love it, I told them. Nearly three hours later we tottered out into the night. Desperate to find something kind to say (there were friends involved), we praised one actor's Jim Carrey imitations and the flashing TV
5 screens all over the postmodern set. And a costume made out of CDs that flashed like disco lights. And one character's use of a mobile phone. The rest was silence.

An American friend walked out of a Globe production recently, claiming that it was insulting her child's intelligence. That sums up the problem of so
10 many contemporary productions; much of the Shakespeare we see now is un-intelligent. The actors can't understand the words and compensate with silly antics. If the protagonist of the play I saw had lain down and kicked his legs in the air one more time, I would have thrown a shoe at him. Directors, unable themselves, I suspect, to understand the text, resort to gimmicks, hiring
15 designers to make the production more 'relevant' or 'meaningful'. [...]. Boredom and Shakespeare go increasingly hand in hand.

At some point during the interminable evening, I found myself thinking the unthinkable: why bother with Shakespeare today? Why not relegate him to the dusty shelves along with Chaucer and the dozens of other Great
20 Unreads in the literary canon? Why are we still so obsessed with Shakespeare that we insist on boring teenagers out of their minds with plays in a language they find foreign? Isn't it time to rethink our relationship with the Bard?

Now, I am not advocating the silly, elitist idea that Shakespeare is so irrelevant to today that students should study the cultural significance of
25 Hollyoaks instead. I believe there is such a thing as great literature, and it is important that every generation should have access to it. I've always been a believer in the importance of Shakespeare for everyone, because not only did he create some of the most wonderful characters ever to grace a stage, but his language is truly marvellous. [...] But my children don't have that language in
30 their heads. All a bad production will do is deter them from going back to Shakespeare in the future.

The problem with Shakespeare today is linguistic. The language has become obsolete, Shakespeare's jokes are meaningless, his witticisms miss their target. It isn't the actors' fault: all they can do is struggle to make sense
35 of a language that might as well be Tibetan. [...]

² **totter** walk unsteadily
¹⁰ **contemporary** [kən'temprəri] *(here)* modern
¹² **antics** stupid behaviour
¹⁴ **resort to sth.** make use of sth. when there is no other solution
¹⁷ **interminable** [ɪn'tɜːmɪnəbl] long and boring
¹⁸ **relegate sth.** ['relɪɡeɪt] move sth.
¹⁹ **Chaucer** English poet (c.1343–1400)
²⁵ **Hollyoaks** popular British TV soap opera
²⁹ **marvellous** great, fantastic
³⁰ **deter sb. from doing sth.** [dɪ'tɜː] make sb. decide not to do sth.
³³ **obsolete** ['ɒbsəliːt ☆ ˌɑːbsə'liːt] no longer used
witticism clever and funny remark

29

Some of the best productions I've seen have not been in English but in German, Spanish, Italian, Japanese and Czech. The plays have been lovingly dissected and translated. The directors don't have to resort to trick lighting and other gimmicks, because the actors understand what they're saying and the audience responds. There is an apocryphal story about a foreign director saying he pitied the English, because they could only read Shakespeare in the original. The other night the full truth of that came home to me. Shakespeare in other languages can have real significance, because people understand him. English audiences can only struggle.

What we need are good English translators to take Shakespeare in hand and liberate him for a new generation. [...] We need to throw away the outdated notion that everyone can understand Shakespeare if only they are exposed to his works, and get down to the business of making sure that people do understand him. Of course, some plays are more accessible than others: some of the tragedies still stand up reasonably well, as do some of the histories. The biggest problem is with the comedies. Maybe that is the best place to start. What we need are two versions of Shakespeare's plays: the original written version for anyone with specialist knowledge of Renaissance English; and the performance version, in good modern English. Shakespeare would doubtless be grateful. What writers want to feel that audiences can't understand their jokes? Please, someone out there, commission a good English translation of Shakespeare and save the Bard from extinction.

From: 'Shakespeare's in danger. We have to act now to avoid a great tragedy', *Independent*, 14 November 2011

38 **dissect sth.** (here) study sth. in detail
40 **apocryphal** [əˈpɒkrɪfl] well known but untrue
41 **pity sb.** feel sorry for sb.
46 **outdated** old-fashioned
56 **commission sth.** officially ask sb. to write or produce sth. for you
57 **extinction** Aussterben

▶ Skill 6: Writing a comment (p. 36)

c Summarize in your own words the main points of the article.

d Identify the text type and the writer's intentions. Point out what devices she uses to achieve her aims and their effect on the reader.

e Analyse the title of this article.

f **EXTRA** Comment on the idea that it is easier for non-English readers to understand Shakespeare.

Skills Support

▶ Skill 1 Doing research

You will often be expected to do research on your own, for example for a presentation or a term paper.

The following steps will help you to use your time and resources effectively:

Step 1: Clarify what your topic is. Write it down in one sentence as if you were explaining it to someone. Make a list of keywords, names, etc. that you want to check on.

Step 2: Start with reference works (e.g. an encyclopedia, Wikipedia, etc.) to get an overview of your topic.

Step 3: The subject catalogue of a well-stocked library will usually lead you most directly to specialized literature. If you are working with an online catalogue or the Internet, use your keywords (Step 1) to locate relevant sources (cf. 'Using the Internet for research' below).

Step 4: Keep in mind that sources vary in their reliability (a book by a university professor is more reliable than an anonymous blog, for example) and that the presentation of the facts in a text can be very one-sided (for example, when a biotech firm defends GM foods).

Step 5: Make notes on all the information that you find relevant for your topic. Using index cards makes it easier to sort the information later.

Step 6: Note your sources carefully (author, title, place and date of publication, publisher; URL if you are using online material). You will need this information later, e.g. in a bibliography, etc.

Using the Internet for research

The Internet has become an indispensable gateway to knowledge. But since anyone can publish on the Internet, you should be particularly careful about your sources.

Another problem is the huge volume of information that can be retrieved. Finding exactly what you are looking for may be a challenge. The following tips can help you.

- Set the preferences (settings) on your search engine to limit results to English-language sources:

    Suchsprache   Wählen Sie eine Sprache aus, um die Suche auf diese Sprache einzugrenzen.
    ○ Suche auf Seiten in jeder beliebigen Sprache
    ● Suche auf Seiten in den folgenden Sprachen eingrenzen:
    ☑ Englisch

- Combine headwords to get the most exact results. For example, you want to collect information on the protest movement against radioactive waste. Googling 'atomic energy' yields ca. 70,000,000 pages; entering 'atomic energy waste protest' reduces the number to ca. 4,000,000.

- Linking headwords with OR produces results with either headword:

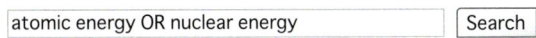

- Use quotation marks to find the exact source of a quote:

- Putting a minus sign in front of a headword excludes it from the results:

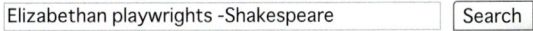

    This search request will yield information that deals mainly with other dramatists of Shakespeare's time.

Skills Support

▶ Skill 2 Giving a presentation

The aim of a presentation is to pass on the most important facts on a topic to the audience in a well-structured and concise way. You will need this skill not only at school, but also in later life (work, college, university, etc.).

Step 1: Planning the content
- Be aware of the time available. Define your topic and limit it to the most important points.
- Research your subject using different sources for greater reliability. ▶ Skill 1 Make notes in English.
- Decide on the relevant information, structure your presentation (introduction, main part, conclusion) and choose examples to support what you are going to say. Plan how much time you can give each point.

Step 2: Preparing the form (practical tips)
- Whether you decide to use a computer and a presentation program, overhead transparencies or something else, layout your texts carefully: use headings or keywords only and make sure they can be seen clearly from the back of the room.
- If you aren't using a presentation program or transparencies, prepare a handout with the main points of your presentation. The handout may also contain additional information, graphs, charts, etc. You may want to leave room for notes.
  - You can either hand it out before or during the presentation to help your audience follow your presentation.
  - Or you can hand it out after the presentation to remind your audience of the main points. In this case, announce the fact that a handout will be distributed at the end so your audience knows that they do not have to take notes and can concentrate on your presentation.
- Visual aids (photos, charts, etc.) will also help your audience to follow your talk, but don't use too many: in order for the visuals to be effective, your audience needs time to look at them.
- Write down what you want to say in keywords on index cards. This will help you to remember your points and to speak freely without reading from the page.
- Look up the pronunciation of difficult words in a dictionary.
- Use the index cards to practise your report until you can deliver it fluently and within the time allowed.
- Even the most attentive audience becomes restless after a while, so
  - use surprising facts or funny anecdotes to keep your audience's attention and
  - **k**eep **i**t **s**hort and **s**imple = **kiss**.
- Remember: Reducing a presentation to the main points takes time and effort, so a presentation given within the time limit is proof of good planning.

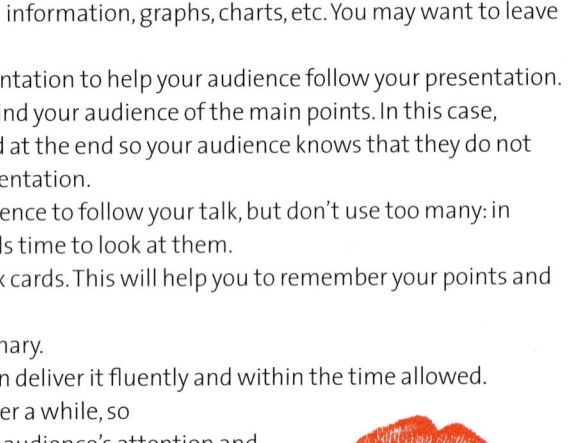
kiss = keep it short and simple

Step 3: Giving the presentation
- Try out the necessary equipment before you start. If you are using music, sound bites or other audio samples, for instance, make sure the speakers are on.
- Begin by stating your topic and how your talk is structured.
- Start with something that will attract and keep the audience's attention.
- Stand up straight, face the audience and speak slowly and clearly.
- Explain any difficult words or expressions.
- Make sure the screen/board/transparencies are visible to everyone. To avoid blocking the view, use a pen or pointer to point out details.
- At the end, summarize the main points and state your conclusion.
- Ask your audience if they have any questions and thank them for their attention.

Skill 3 Reading poetry

▶ Glossary (pp. 44–48)

Interpreting poetry means
a) *identifying the theme, the speaker, the formal elements and the use of language,*
b) *showing how these aspects contribute to the overall effect of the poem and*
c) *showing how effective they are in conveying the message or meaning of the poem to the reader.*

Step 1: Read the poem two or three times, also aloud if it helps, or until you feel you have understood it. Then consider
- its theme or topic and/or the event or situation presented in the poem;
- what sort of poem it is: descriptive, narrative or something else;
- the speaker (if there is one) and who (if anybody) the speaker is addressing;
- the link between the poem and its title;
- the intention of the poem.

Step 2: Examine how the poem is composed by looking at the formal elements. To determine what type of poem it is (ballad, sonnet, ode, hymn, etc.), consider
- the number of stanzas;
- the rhyme scheme (if there is one);
- the effect of the rhythm and the rhyme scheme (if there is one) and
- whether any unexpected changes in rhythm or rhyme scheme emphasize the importance of a particular line or passage.

Step 3: Analyse the language in the poem and decide
- whether it is simple or more complex;
- whether there are any repetitions or contrasts and, if so, what effect they have;
- whether imagery is used and what effect it has;

Step 4: Interpret the poem. A written interpretation consists of three parts: an introduction, a body and a conclusion.

- Introduction:
  – Mention the title, the poet and the theme of the poem as well as your findings from Step 1.
  - **Language help 1**

Language help 1
- The poem ... by ... deals with / is about ...
- In the poem ... describes / thinks about / reflects on ...
- The poet speaks to / addresses the reader directly in order to ...
- The title refers to / reminds the reader of ...

- Body:
  – Use your findings from Steps 2 and 3 to explain how the poem conveys its message.
  – Name the stylistic devices and explain how and why they are used.
  - **Language help 2**

Language help 2
- The poem is made up / composed of ...
- The poem follows the rhyme scheme .... This creates an impression of ...
- The poet ignores the traditional rhyme schemes in order to ...
- The imagery conveys a sense of ...
- The imagery is used to .... This makes the poem particularly effective.
- Line ... runs into line ... which emphasizes ...
- The language is simple/formal/complex, which intensifies the feeling of ...

- Conclusion:
  – State whether you think the poem is effective.
  - **Language help 3**

Language help 3
- All in all / In general / The overall effect is ...
- The rhythm / ... contributes to ...
- The poem succeeds in showing/conveying/expressing ...

Skills Support

▶ Skill 4 Reading/Watching drama

▶ Glossary (pp. 44–48)

A drama or play is a fictional text in which a dramatist presents actions, settings and characters to be performed on stage, as a film or on the radio. It is important to bear this in mind when reading a play and to try and picture the stage, the characters and how they play their roles, and how the audience is involved.

'It stinks!'

Step 1: When analysing a play, consider the following aspects:
- The acts and scenes:
  - How does the dramatist use these divisions in the play? Do they correspond to action, time, place or a combination of these?
- The stage directions:
  - How helpful are they (when reading) for imagining the setting, characters, etc.?
- The language and the dramatic dialogue:
  - How does the language reflect the social status of the characters?
  - Why did/didn't the dramatist use conversational language?
  - What is the function of the dialogue: to move the action forward, give information about the characters or describe the setting? Or does it serve another function?
- The reader/audience:
  - Is anything left to the reader's/audience's imagination?
  - What does the reader/audience know that the character does not know? (The character's words may have a different meaning for the audience than for the character. This is called dramatic irony; it gets the reader/audience more involved.)

Step 2: When talking about the play, use language which makes it clear you are analysing a fictional drama and not talking about real life.
- Language help 1

Step 3: Say not only what the play is about but also what the author's intention might be.
- Language help 2

Step 4: When looking at the characters, consider what they say themselves, what other characters say about them and how they are presented on stage.
- Language help 3

Language help 1
- In his/her play the dramatist is concerned with the topic/subject/issue ...
- He/She has divided his/her play into ... acts, which correspond to ...
- The development of the action corresponds with the play's division into acts and scenes.
- He/She makes the social differences between the characters clear by ...

Language help 2
- In the play a conflict develops between ... and ..., who could be seen as representing/standing for ...
- The play does not draw a definite conclusion, which suggests that the dramatist did not want to present solutions to the problems/conflicts shown in the play.

Language help 3
- Although Y sees himself/herself as a friendly character, the way he/she behaves towards Z shows that ...
- Y is described as being ... but his/her language reveals him/her to be ...

Skill 5 Writing an essay

When writing an essay, you are required to present a topic in a coherent way, for example by presenting arguments for and against a topic.

Step 1: Read the task carefully and pay particular attention to the special vocabulary used in tasks, so that you know exactly what is required of you.

Step 2: Proceed as you would with any other text, from first draft to final draft giving yourself enough time to re-read your essay and check for grammar and spelling mistakes, but consider the following points as well:

- In your introduction restate the problem from your task. You can also state your main points and explain the structure of your text.
- Present your arguments in the main part of your essay. Devote one paragraph to each of the arguments. Use connectors to make your text coherent. ■ **Language help**
- If you are asked to analyse or examine an issue, arrange your arguments according to their importance, from the weakest to the strongest point or vice versa.
- If you are asked to discuss a topic, i.e. weigh up the pros and cons, you can take the argumentative approach and deal with all the arguments in favour of the topic first and then all the arguments against the topic next. Alternatively, you can discuss one aspect at a time, presenting ideas for and against each aspect one after the other.
- If you are asked to compare two things, deal with the similarities first and then the differences or vice versa.
- Make a concluding statement in which you sum up your arguments.

> **Language help**
>
> ■ *Stating your opinion*
>   In my opinion ... / To my mind ... / I think/feel/believe ...
> ■ *Enumerating facts, etc.:*
>   a) *starting*
>   Firstly ... / First of all ... / For one thing ...
>   b) *continuing*
>   Secondly ... / Furthermore ... / Moreover ... / Besides ... / Also ... / In addition (to) ... / As well as ... / Another point is ...
>   c) *finishing*
>   Above all ... / Finally ...
> ■ *Giving an example*
>   ... for example ... / ... for instance ... / ... such as ... / ..., say, ...
> ■ *Pointing out reasons or consequences*
>   For this reason ... / For these reasons ... / Due to ... / Because of ... / As a result (of) ... / Consequently ... / As a consequence ... / Therefore ... / So ... / That explains why ...
> ■ *Emphasizing*
>   In fact ... / As a matter of fact ... / In reality ...
> ■ *Contrasting*
>   On the one hand ... on the other hand ... / However ... / Nonetheless ... / At first ... but then ... / Although ... / In spite of ... / Whereas ...
> ■ *Conceding a point*
>   Of course ... / To be sure ... / Admittedly ...
> ■ *Pointing out a restriction or objection*
>   Still ... / After all ...
> ■ *Referring to a point in time or a development*
>   At that time ... / In those days ...
>   Eventually ... / In the long run ... / In the course of time ..., Meanwhile ... / At the same time ...
> ■ *Coming to a conclusion*
>   All in all ... / Ultimately ... / In the final analysis ... / In conclusion ..., For the reasons mentioned above ... To sum up ... / To conclude ...
>   I would like to conclude by saying that ...

'And this student model is programmed with the answers to 500 popular essay questions.'

Skills Support

▶ Skill 6 Writing a comment

The aim of a comment is to demonstrate that you are able to present your opinion on a certain topic in a coherent form.

Step 1: Read the task carefully and make sure you know what is required of you. Form your opinion on the topic.

Step 2: Collect and group arguments and examples to support your opinion – either in a mind map or as an outline. This way you have an overview of what you want to say, and you can plan your introduction.

Step 3: Make an introductory statement in which you rouse the reader's interest and refer to the task. Give your general opinion on the topic and outline reasons for your opinion.

Step 4: Devote one paragraph to each of the arguments you want to present. Illustrate your arguments with appropriate examples.

Step 5: Make your concluding statement, in which you sum up your opinion and your arguments.

Language help
- I am of the opinion that ... / I take the view that ...
- As far as I understand / can see ...
- I think/believe/suppose ...
- I am sure/convinced/certain that ...
- There are many reasons for ... / There is no doubt that ...

▶ Skill 7 Writing a review

A review is a written text that aims at providing information, usually about a book, film or play. It is intended either to recommend the work in question or to discourage people from reading or seeing it. It can also help people to form their own opinion about the work.

Step 1: Prepare yourself by considering the various elements which make up a fictional or non-fictional text, a film or a play. ▶ Skill 4

Step 2: Say what the book, film or play is about, giving the title, genre, name of the writer, director, etc. and when it was written, made, etc.

Step 3: Give background information on the book, film or play and on the author, director or playwright.

Step 4: Give specific information on what the book, film or play is about and provide a short summary but try not to give the ending away (unless this is explicitly required). You can also present a short extract that is typical of the work you are reviewing, but not essential to understanding the whole work. You should aim to make your audience curious and encourage them to read or watch the work themselves rather than give everything away.

Step 5: Finish your review with your personal opinion about the book, film or play, give reasons for your opinion and say whether you would recommend the work or not.

Language help
- ... was written by ... / ... is a novel/film/play by ...
- The novel/film/play is set in / covers a period of / tells the story of ...
- The main characters are ...
- The novel is beautifully/awfully written.
- I can thoroughly recommend the novel/film/play ...
- The story is rather weak/boring/unconvincing.

Active Vocabulary

Vocabulary you should learn (from pages 6–22)

Lead-in

p.7	**lad** *(old-fashioned or infml)*	= a boy or young man	*Bursche, Knabe, Jüngling*

Words in Context:
Shakespeare, His Theatre and His Time

p.8	**(to) be rated as** sth.	*synonyms:* (to) be regarded as sth. / (to) be considered to be sth.	*als etwas gelten*
	playwright ['pleɪraɪt]	= someone who writes plays for a living	*Bühnenschriftsteller/in, Stückeschreiber/in*
	comedy ['kɒmədi]	Shakespeare's **~ies** still make people laugh today.	*Komödie*
	tragedy ['trædʒədi]	Shakespeare's **~ies** often end with the death of the main characters.	*Tragödie*
	history (play)	Shakespeare's **history ~s** depict the lives of the historical kings and queens of England.	*Historiendrama*
	the Elizabethan Age [ɪˌlɪzəˈbiːθən]	The **~ Age** is associated with the reign of Queen Elizabeth I in England from 1558 to 1603.	*das Elisabethanische Zeitalter*
	golden age	= a period of peace, prosperity and progress in a country	*Goldenes Zeitalter; Blütezeit*
	achievement in the arts [əˈtʃiːvmənt]	The play was the greatest **~ in the ~** during that time.	*künstlerische Errungenschaft*
	(to) struggle for sth. [ˈstrʌɡl]	King Charles I famously **~d for** power with the English Parliament during his reign.	*um etwas ringen*
	threat from foreign powers [θret, ˈfɒrən]	The monarch has received a **~ from foreign ~**.	*von fremden Mächten ausgehende (Be-)Drohung*
	traditional world view [vjuː]	The **~ world ~** held in the Middle Ages was that the earth was flat.	*traditionelle Weltanschauung*
	old dogma [ˈdɒɡmə]	= old beliefs, which people are expected to accept without question	*altes Dogma, alte unumstößliche Lehrmeinung*
	master of his own fate [ˈmɑːstə]	= someone who has control over the direction their life takes	*seines eigenen Glückes Schmied*
	predetermined [ˌpriːdɪˈtɜːmɪnd]	*synonym:* predestined [ˌpriːˈdestɪnd]	*vorherbestimmt*
	profit [ˈprɒfɪt ☆ ˈprɑːfɪt]	If the theatre is full, you know the producer has made a **~**.	*Gewinn, Profit*

Active Vocabulary

(p.8)	**upheaval** [ʌpˈhiːvl]	The Middle Ages were a time of religious and social ~.	*Umbruch, Umwälzung, Aufruhr*
	(to) invest in sth. [ɪnˈvest]	*word family:* (to) **invest** – investor – investment	*in etwas investieren*
	(to) produce a play [prəˈdjuːs]	Peter Brook famously ~d Shakespeare's ~ *A Midsummer Night's Dream* in the 1970's.	*ein Theaterstück aufführen/inszenieren*
	a popular form of entertainment [ˌentəˈteɪnmənt]	Since the invention of television, theatre is no longer the most **popular form of** ~.	*eine beliebte Art der Unterhaltung*
	(to) draw sb. (to a show)	= (to) tempt or attract sb. (to a show)	*(Zuschauer, Besucher usw.) anziehen / (in eine Vorstellung) locken*
	spectator [spekˈteɪtə ☆ ˈspekteɪtər]	The ~s at plays in Shakespeare's day typically became very rowdy.	*Zuschauer/in*
	playhouse [ˈpleɪhaʊs]	The Liverpool **P**~ traditionally shows productions of old plays.	*Schauspielhaus, Theater*
	open to the sky	theatres which are **open to the** ~ = open-air theatres	*zum Himmel hin offen*
	stage [steɪdʒ]	= the platform on which the action of a play takes place	*Bühne*
	scenery [ˈsiːnəri]	The ~ really made me believe I was in a forest in England!	*Bühnenbild, Kulisse*
	performance [pəˈfɔːməns]	*word family:* (to) perform – performer – **performance**	*Aufführung, Vorführung*
	speech	His ~ was far too quiet. I couldn't hear one word!	*hier: Sprechweise*
	expression [ɪkˈspreʃn]	*word family:* (to) express sth. – expressive – **expression**	*Ausdruck*
	gesture [ˈdʒestʃə]	He ought to have used more ~s to express the tragedy of the scene.	*Gestik, Geste*
	(to) hold the crowd's attention [kraʊd, əˈtenʃn]	A good play can ~ for hours.	*die Aufmerksamkeit des Publikums aufrechterhalten*
	(to) learn one's lines	He forgot his words because he hadn't ~ ~ properly.	*seinen (Rollen-)Text lernen, seine Rolle lernen*
	transcript [ˈtrænskrɪpt]	I've got a ~ of the wrong play! I can't learn my lines.	*Abschrift, Kopie*
	role	Who is in the leading ~ of this production of *Othello*?	*(Bühnen-)Rolle; Part*
	dialogue [ˈdaɪəlɒg]	The ~ between Romeo and Juliet was so romantic.	*Dialog*
	monologue [ˈmɒnəlɒg]	= a long speech spoken by only one character in a play or film	*Monolog*
	character [ˈkærəktə]	Hermia and Helena are two of the major ~s in the play.	*Figur, Gestalt (in Buch, Film usw.)*

Active Vocabulary

(p.8)	**stage directions** [dəˈrekʃnz]	= instructions given to actors in a play telling them what to do	*Bühnenanweisungen*
	replica [ˈreplɪkə]	This room is an exact ~ of Shakespeare's study.	*Nachbau; Reproduktion, Kopie*
	antiquated [ˈæntɪkweɪtɪd]	*synonyms:* outdated / old-fashioned	*veraltet, überholt*
	theme [θiːm]	Love is the central ~ of *A Midsummer Night's Dream*.	*(immer wiederkehrendes) Thema; Leitmotiv*
	timeless [ˈtaɪmləs]	The design of this beautiful building is ~.	*zeitlos*

Part B: Drama

B1 Love: A Midsummer Night's Dream

p.12	(to) **desire** sb. [dɪˈzaɪə]	*word family:* (to) **desire** – desire *(n)* – desirable	*jdn. begehren*
p.13	**modesty** [ˈmɒdəsti]	She has no ~; she always talks about her achievements!	*Sittsamkeit, Anstand; Bescheidenheit*
	supernatural [ˌsuːpəˈnætʃrəl]	Many people still believe in the ~ world of fairies and magic.	*übersinnlich, übernatürlich*

B2 Power and Ambition: Julius Caesar

p.14	(to) **assassinate** sb. [əˈsæsɪneɪt]	*word family:* (to) **assassinate** – assassination – assassin	*jdn. ermorden*

B3 Revenge: Othello

p.16	**revenge** [rɪˈvendʒ]	She will take ~ on her enemies for treating her badly.	*Rache*
	envy *(n)* [ˈenvi]	*word family:* **envy** – (to) envy – envious – enviable	*Neid*

Part C: Versions of Shakespeare

C3 Sonnets and the German Shakespeare

p.20	**outcast** *(adj)* [ˈaʊtkɑːst]	She felt ~ in a country where nobody spoke her language.	*ausgestoßen*

Word Help

Selected vocabulary from the accompanying audios and videos to assist comprehension

p. 18 | **C1** DVD Comparing Two Shakespeare Productions   Task 2: Comparing performances

1. Stage Version 1970

villain [ˈvɪlən]	a person who is morally bad or responsible for causing trouble or harm
(to) **conjure** sth. **up** [ˈkʌndʒə]	(to) make sth. appear as a picture in your mind
(to) **debase** sb./sth.	(to) reduce the value of sb./sth.
(to) **languish** (in sth.) *(fml)* [ˈlæŋgwɪʃ]	(to) suffer hardship or distress for a long time
ounce [aʊns]	a unit for measuring weight (1 ounce = 28.35 grams)
pard	leopard
boar = wild boar [bɔː]	a wild pig
vile	extremely unpleasant or bad
rehearsal [rɪˈhɜːsl]	the act of practising sth., for example a play, in preparation for a public perfomance
collaboration (with sb.**) (on** sth.**)** [kəˌlæbəˈreɪʃn]	the act of working together with sb. or a group of people to create sth.

2. BBC production: Shakespeare retold

nightingale	a small bird that sings very beautifully, esp. at night
female attention	interest shown by women
(to) **play second headline**	(to) perform (music, comedy) at a club before the main act
fair share	gerechter Anteil, angemessene Beteiligung
fanny *(BE, taboo, sl)*	female sex organs
gift of the gab	the ability to talk a lot without feeling shy
rough [rʌf]	rude, uncultured, tough
(to) **hang around**	(to) wait or stay near a place, not doing very much
gorgeous [ˈgɔːdʒəs]	very beautiful or pleasant
handmaiden *(old-fashioned)*	a female servant
(to) **be bang on** *(infml)*	(to) be exactly right
(to) **wait on** sb.	(to) act as a servant to sb., esp. by serving food to them
rash	Hautausschlag
(to) **fall for** sth.	(to) believe that a trick or a joke is true

Word Help

stag night *(BE)*	the night when a group of men celebrate together because one of them is soon to be married
bookie *(infml)*	= bookmaker (= sb. who takes bets from people on the result of a race or competition, and pays them if they win)
(to) **get out of hand**	(to) get out of control
(to) **lead** sb. **up and down**	(to) tell sb. exactly what to do
theme tune [ˈθiːm tjuːn]	Titelmelodie, Erkennungsmelodie
a head squeeze	a confusing situation
(to) **get your head squeezed**	here: (to) get beaten up

p.25 **Further Practice, A1–A4** `CD 05–06` Task 3: Shakespeare in Stratford

Part 1

staging of sth.	putting sth. on stage
thrust stage	a platform stage, i.e. extending into the audience on three sides
in tandem [ˈtæmdəm]	parallel to each other

Part 2

good box office	popular, attracting large audiences
(to) **hold** sb. **in high esteem** [ɪˈstiːm]	(to) respect sb. highly
messy	untidy, chaotic
rude [ruːd]	vulgar, impolite, primitive
coherence [kəʊˈhɪərəns]	a situation where all the parts of sth. fit together well

Shakespearean English

Early Modern English

The Elizabethan Age was a time of great innovation and progress: major changes in social, political, scientific, as well as linguistic fields took place during this period. It was during this time that Early Modern English *(= Frühneuenglisch)* developed. The language contained a huge variety of words of different origin (Anglo-Saxon, French, Latin, etc.) and had an extremely flexible grammatical structure and rules for spelling. Even the spelling of names was not fixed: 'Shakespeare' as we write it today was only canonized[1] in the 19th century.

[1] **canonize sb.** [ˈkænənaɪz] jdn. heiligsprechen *(hier: die Schreibung „Shakespeare" einheitlich festlegen)*

Shakespeare's words and grammar

Shakespeare made verbs out of nouns *(to child)*, created opposites by using prefixes *(to unsex, to unchild)* or simply made up words for the sound of them *(hurly-burly, hugger-mugger, kickie-wickie)*. However, not all the words that are associated with him, e.g. in the Oxford English Dictionary, were really invented by him – he just wrote many of them down for the first time. A great number of them have since become idioms or sayings in the English language.

Aspects which can make reading and understanding Shakespeare challenging include the following:

- Some words have completely disappeared *(forsooth* = honestly; *aye* = yes; *thou* = you).
- Others have now acquired[2] a different meaning from what they meant in Shakespeare's time *(pregnant* = full of, clever; *silly* = innocent; *fat* = glistening with sweat).
- There were no fixed rules concerning word order *(to yon cart was our horse hitched)*.
- Some verbs still had archaic[3] endings *(thou hast; thou dost; he hath; thou art)*.
- Words or syllables could be left out, sometimes due to the metre* *(e'en* [iːn] = even; *ne'er* [neə] = never; *we will to bed)*.

[2] **acquire sth.** *(fml)* etwas erwerben

[3] **archaic** [ɑːˈkeɪɪk] veraltet, altertümlich

Shakespeare used all the opportunities that this 'new' language gave him, because in his day the emphasis of theatre was usually on hearing rather than watching a play. The effect of his play therefore had to be created largely by words rather than by anything else.

Some well-known quotes from Shakespeare's plays

A horse! A horse! My kingdom for a horse! (from: **Richard III**)
Ein Pferd! Ein Pferd! Mein Königreich für ein Pferd!

Nothing can come of nothing. (from: **King Lear**)
Von nichts kommt nichts.

To be, or not to be – that is the question. (from: **Hamlet**)
Sein oder Nichtsein – das ist hier die Frage.

Much Ado About Nothing (comedy title)
Viel Lärm um nichts

There are more things in heaven and earth than are dreamt of in your philosophy. (from: **Hamlet**)
Es gibt mehr Dinge im Himmel und auf Erden, als Eure Schulweisheit sich träumt.

Well roared, lion! (from: **A Midsummer Night's Dream**)
Gut gebrüllt, Löwe!

All the world's a stage, and all the men and women merely players. (from: **As You Like It**)
Die ganze Welt ist eine Bühne und alle Frauen und Männer bloße Spieler.

Shakespeare's Work in German

The relationship between Shakespeare and Germany has always been a fruitful, but also controversial one. In the beginning, Shakespeare's plays came to Germany as puppet[1] theatre. Shakespeare in the original and in translation provided an example for many German writers and encouraged the development of a genuinely[2] German national literature.

[1] **puppet** Handpuppe, Marionette
[2] **genuinely** ['dʒenjuɪnli] echt, wirklich

The classical German Shakespeare

Not until 1741 *(Julius Caesar)* and 1758 *(Romeo and Juliet)* were the first plays translated into German. From 1762 to 1766 Christoph Martin Wieland published the first more or less complete edition with the help of a French-English dictionary. The most famous German version is probably the so-called 'Schlegel-Tieck' translation (1797 to 1840), which is still performed on stages today. Yet their translation was not the product of their partnership, as the name would suggest, but rather the subject of a long-term argument between the writers. Nevertheless, Schlegel, Tieck, Tieck's sister Dorothea and a friend called Baudissin produced the classical German Shakespeare.

Brutus:
  Another general shout!
  I do believe that these applauses are
  For some new honours that are heaped on Caesar.
Cassius:
  Why, man, he doth bestride the narrow world
  Like a Colossus; and we petty men
  Walk under his huge legs and peep about
  To find ourselves dishonourable graves.
  Men at some time are masters of their fates:
  The fault, dear Brutus, is not in our stars
  But in ourselves, that we are underlings.
  Brutus and Caesar: what should be in that 'Caesar'?
  Why should that name be sounded more than yours?
  Write them together, yours is as fair a name;
  Sound them, it doth become the mouth as well;
  Weigh them, it is as heavy; conjure with 'em,
  'Brutus' will start a spirit as soon as 'Caesar'.

Brutus:
  Ein neues Jauchzen!
  Ich glaube, dieser Beifall gilt die Ehren,
  Die man auf Cäsars Haupt von neuem häuft.
Cassius:
  Ja, er beschreitet, Freund, die enge Welt
  Wie ein Colossus, und wir kleinen Leute,
  Wir wandeln unter seinen Riesenbeinen,
  Und schaun umher nach einem schnöden Grab.
  Der Mensch ist manchmal seines Schicksals Meister:
  Nicht durch die Schuld der Sterne, lieber Brutus,
  Durch eigne Schuld nur sind wir Schwächlinge.
  Brutus und Cäsar – was steckt doch in dem Cäsar,
  Dass man den Namen mehr als Euren spräche?
  Schreibt sie zusammen: ganz so schön ist Eurer;
  Sprecht sie: er steht den Lippen ganz so wohl;
  Wägt sie: er ist so schwer; beschwört mit ihnen:
  Brutus ruft Geister auf so schnell wie Cäsar.

From: *Julius Cäsar*, translated by August Wilhelm von Schlegel

Translations and more

To date, Shakespeare's complete works have been reproduced in German at least 40 times, along with countless other versions of individual plays. Examples include writers and translators such as Rudolf Alexander Schröder with his baroque Shakespeare, and Erich Fried or Frank Günther in contemporary times. The sonnets* in particular have interested many German writers and translators, resulting in at least 200 translations, including more than 60 translations of the complete cycle.

Glossary

1 Drama/Play

- **Dramas** (or **plays**) are not written to be read but to be performed by **actors** on **stage** in a theatre and watched by an audience.

- A play is usually divided into several **acts**, and the acts may be subdivided into **scenes**. In classical drama, there were usually five acts, but modern plays normally consist of three and sometimes only of one act.

- The essential element of all plays is the **characters**, the people in the play. Good plays show us a lot about their feelings and emotions in the situations in which they find themselves. Characters also usually change during the play – they develop.

  Drama means 'tension' – often conflict between characters.

  We find out what is happening in plays by what the characters say, and we often have to read between the lines in order to understand a situation. Plays also use spoken language which can, for example, include slang and other informal ways of speaking.

- A **soliloquy** [sə'lıləkwiː] *(= Monolog)* is a speech made by a character in a play in which his or her thoughts, emotions or motives are revealed.

- **Stage directions** are the written instructions of a play explaining how it should be performed, e.g. a description of its setting, movements or actions of the characters, the sound or lighting, etc. This helps the actors perform a play.

> **Some of the stage directions in Shakespeare's plays**
> **enter …** instruction telling one or more characters to come on stage
> **re-enter …** instruction telling one or more characters to come on stage again
> **exit …** ['eksɪt, 'egzɪt] instruction telling a character to leave the stage
> **exeunt …** ['eksiʌnt] instruction telling two or more characters to leave the stage
> **flourish** ['flʌrɪʃ ☆ 'flɜːrɪʃ] music (e.g. a short trumpet passage) introducing the entrance or exit of a king or another important person

⚠ **Trouble spot**
happy end**ing**
Not: happy end

Types of drama

- A **comedy** is a type of drama which deals with a topic in an amusing way. It always has a happy ending.

- A **tragedy** is a type of drama in which the protagonist goes through a series of misfortunes that finally lead to his or her downfall. This downfall is usually brought about by the **protagonists** themselves, e.g. through pride or weakness.

Glossary

2 Poetry

- A **poem** is a piece of creative writing structured by **lines** and **rhythm** (the arrangement of stressed and unstressed syllables in a line). The lines of a poem are often arranged into groups called **stanzas**. To emphasize the structure and to create certain effects, traditional poets frequently make use of rhyme. Modern poetry often uses **free verse**, which makes little use of rhyme. The poetry comes from **repetition**, **imagery** and the arrangement of words and stresses in the poem.

- Poems are often **lyrical** (i.e. they express personal thoughts and feelings), but they can also be **narrative** (i.e. they tell a story).

- The **speaker of a poem** (= *lyrisches Ich*) is the fictional person who speaks the text of a poem. In theory, the speaker is not identical to the writer;

- **Rhyme** is the similarity of sounds between certain words (especially stressed syllables), usually at the end of lines. When identifying the **rhyme scheme** (i.e. which words at the end of the lines rhyme), it is usual to use small letters to indicate that words share a rhyme. If the words *abide*, *thee*, *wide* and *see* occur respectively at the end of four successive lines, the rhyme scheme is written as a b a b. This pattern is called **alternate** [ɔːlˈtɜːnət] **rhyme** (= *Kreuzreim*). If *abide*, *wide*, *thee* and *see* occur respectively at the end of four successive lines, the rhyme scheme is written a a b b. This pattern is called **rhyming couplets** [ˈkʌpləts] (= *Paarreim*).

- **Metre** (AE: **meter**) is the regular rhythm of the words in a poem. Traditionally, this is achieved by the arrangement of stressed and unstressed syllables in the line of a poem. The most common metre in English is the **iambic pentameter** [aɪˌæmbɪk penˈtæmɪtə], which consists of a line of five feet (each **foot** consists of an unstressed syllable followed by a stressed syllable).

- **Poetic language:** poems are generally short compared to stories and plays, but the writer (the **poet**) wants to say a lot in a few lines. To do this, he or she often uses language in a very special way so that the words have a strong effect on the reader. There are usually lots of **stylistic devices** (▶ pp. 46–47), and **images** are particularly important in poems.

- A **sonnet** [ˈsɒnɪt] is a poem consisting of 14 lines. Sonnets became popular in England in the 17th century and were used mostly for love poetry, but later they came to embrace a wide number of themes. There are various types of sonnets: Shakespeare's sonnets comprised three **quatrains** [ˈkwɒtreɪnz] (a quatrain consists of four lines with a shared rhyme scheme) and a **couplet** (i.e. two successive lines which rhyme). As the couplet's rhyme scheme was different from the rest of the sonnet it was used to sum up or vary or change the theme of the sonnet.

> ⚠ **Trouble spot**
> English 'sonnet'
> = German „Sonett"

Glossary

3 Stylistic devices

When you analyse a text, you may be asked to point out any stylistic devices used by the writer. These are special ways of using language and particularly common in speeches and most fictional texts. Several of the terms come from Greek or Latin.

alliteration [əˌlɪtəˈreɪʃn]	Alliteration, Stabreim	Repeating a sound (usually a consonant) at the beginnings of words that are next to each other. The effect is to make e.g. a line of poetry more interesting and beautiful as language: *(Imagine all the people) living life in peace.*
allusion [əˈluːʒn]	Anspielung	Making a direct or indirect reference to a person or a thing that the reader recognizes and responds to. The effect is to stress that this person or thing has something in common with the topic you are talking about and to make the reader feel like an insider, like a person who shares certain knowledge with the writer.
antithesis [ænˈtɪθəsɪs]	Antithese, Gegensatz	Putting two ideas close together so that there is a clear contrast. The effect is to emphasize just how different the two ideas are: *If you don't know how to fix it, stop breaking it!*
assonance [ˈæsənəns]	Assonanz, Halbreim	Repeating the same vowel sound in successive words. The effect is to bind these sentences together by using a similar sound.
cliché [ˈkliːʃeɪ ☆ kliːˈʃeɪ]	Klischee	Using an expression which has been used too much and therefore seems boring, meaningless or unoriginal. The effect can be humorous (if the writer uses it knowing full well that this expression is dated), but it may also indicate that the writer is not very original.
comparison [kəmˈpærɪsn]	Vergleich	Comparing two or more people or things. A comparison highlights particular similarities and/or differences between the people/things in question.
contrast [ˈkɒntrɑːst ☆ ˈkɑːntræst]	Gegensatz, Kontrast	Bringing together opposing views or characters in order to emphasize their difference. For example the writer may introduce a very bad character to stress the goodness of another. The effect is to illustrate how different the two aspects are.
enumeration [ɪˌnjuːməˈreɪʃn]	Aufzählung	Listing words, phrases or ideas. The effect is to emphasize the things listed or to make the text easier to read.
euphemism [ˈjuːfəmɪzəm]	Euphemismus	Expressing something embarrassing or unpleasant in a gentler way. The effect is to make something appear less negative.
exaggeration [ɪɡˌzædʒəˈreɪʃn]/ **hyperbole** [haɪˈpɜːbəli]	Übertreibung/ Hyperbel	Making a person, action, etc. seem bigger or more important than in reality. The effect is to emphasize something (often in an amusing way): *I am so tired I could sleep for a year!*
exclamation [ˌekskləˈmeɪʃn]	Ausruf, Aufschrei	A short word or phrase spoken suddenly to express an emotion. The effect is usually rather abrupt and dramatic.
imagery [ˈɪmɪdʒəri]	Metaphorik, Sprachbilder	Expressing an idea through an **image** – a mental picture. It allows the reader/listener to 'see' an abstract idea in a concrete way, and so understand it better: *His face was like a red tomato. I'm drowning in a sea of problems.*

Glossary

■ **metaphor** [ˈmetəfə ☆ -fɔːr]	*Metapher*	A comparison that is made without using the words *as* or *like*. Something is directly described as being something else. Writers use metaphors to create an image in the reader's mind, to make their texts more illustrative.
■ **simile** [ˈsɪməli]	*Vergleich*	A comparison between things. While a metaphor says that something <u>is</u> something else, a simile says that something <u>is like</u> something else, and it does use words like *as* or *like*. Like metaphors, similes help to illustrate ideas.
■ **symbol** [ˈsɪmbl]	*Symbol, Zeichen*	A thing, word or phrase that does not only stand for itself, but also for a certain abstract idea. E.g. the dove is a symbol of peace.
■ **personification** [pəˌsɒnɪfɪˈkeɪʃn]	*Personifizierung*	Presenting an animal or object like a human being.
irony [ˈaɪrəni]	*Ironie*	Saying the opposite of what you really think. The effect is to criticize something heavily, or to make something look ridiculous. A text which uses irony to make fun of an institution or person, etc. is called a piece of **satire** [ˈsætaɪə].
juxtaposition [ˌdʒʌkstəpəˈzɪʃn]	*Gegenüberstellung*	A very strong contrast of opposing ideas, arguments, views, mostly introduced by words like *but, however, nevertheless*.
onomatopoeia [ˌɒnəˌmætəˈpiːə]	*Lautmalerei*	Using words that imitate the sound they refer to, e.g. *buzz* or *hum*. The effect is to create a certain mood, feeling or movement.
paradox [ˈpærədɒks ☆ -dɑːks]		A statement that seems impossible because it contains two opposing ideas that are both true. *In this rich country, there is a lot of poverty.*
parallelism [ˈpærəlelɪzəm]	*Parallelismus, Parallelität*	Deliberately repeating similar or identical words, phrases, sentence constructions, etc. in the same or neighbouring sentences.
repetition [ˌrepəˈtɪʃn]	*Wiederholung*	Saying the same thing many times. There are two main ways in which writers repeat words or phrases in a text. Both (a) help to structure a list of ideas, and (b) emphasize key ideas:
■ **anaphora** [əˈnæfərə]	*Anapher*	Repetition at the beginning of a sentence or part of a sentence: *It was the best of times, it was the worst of times, it was the age of wisdom, it was the age of foolishness.*
■ **epiphora** [ɪˈpɪfərə]	*Epipher*	Repetition at the end of a sentence or part of a sentence: *Here a cousin, there a cousin, everywhere we turned, a kissing cousin was puckering up at us.*
rhetorical question [rɪˈtɒrɪkl]	*rhetorische Frage*	Asking a question to which everyone already knows the answer. In speeches, this is a way of saying something with strong effect: *Do you want war? Do you want hunger in the world? Do you want injustice?* (The clear answer is: *No!*)
understatement / litotes [laɪˈtəʊtiːz]	*Untertreibung / Litotes*	Making a person, action, situation, etc. seem smaller / less important than in reality (▶ exaggeration). The effect is, in fact, to show just the opposite – how big or important something is: *(Captain of a plane that is about to crash:)* 'Ladies and gentlemen, we have a small problem.'
wordplay / pun / play on words	*Wortspiel*	Using a word that can be understood in two different ways. The effect can be to draw attention to the two meanings or to create humour.

Glossary

Alphabetical list of terms in the Glossary

act p.44
actor p.44
alliteration p.46
allusion p.46
alternate rhyme p.45
anaphora p.47
antithesis p.46
assonance p.46
character p.44
cliché p.46
comedy p.44
comparison p.46
contrast p.46
couplet p.45
drama p.44
enumeration p.46
epiphora p.47

euphemism p.46
exaggeration p.46
exclamation p.46
foot p.45
free verse p.45
hyperbole p.46
iambic pentameter p.45
image pp.45, 46
imagery pp.45, 46
irony p.47
juxtaposition p.47
line p.45
litotes p.47
lyrical p.45
metaphor p.47
metre p.45

narrative p.45
onomatopoeia p.47
paradox p.47
parallelism p.47
personification p.47
play p.44
play on words p.47
poem p.45
poet p.45
poetic language p.45
protagonist p.44
pun p.47
quatrain p.45
repetition pp.45, 47
rhetorical question p.47
rhyme p.45
rhyme scheme p.45

rhyming couplet p.45
rhythm p.45
satire p.47
scene p.44
simile p.47
soliloquy p.44
sonnet p.45
speaker of a poem p.45
stage p.44
stage directions p.44
stanza p.45
stylistic device p.45
symbol p.47
tragedy p.44
understatement p.47
wordplay p.47

'I didn't feel answers were necessary. All the questions seemed rhetorical.'